SHOCK WAVE 2000!

Harold Camping's 1994 Debacle

SHOCK WAVE 2000!

Harold Camping's 1994 Debacle

Robert A. Sungenis
Scott Temple
David Allen Lewis

New Leaf Press

First Printing: August 1994

Copyright © 1994 by New Leaf Press. All rights reserved. Printed in the United States of America. No part of this book may be used or reproduced in any manner whatsoever without written permission of the publisher except in the case of brief quotations in articles and reviews. For information write: New Leaf Press, Inc., P.O. Box 311, Green Forest, AR 72638.

ISBN: 0-89221-269-1
Library of Congress: 94-67493

Contents

Foreword

The history of the Church has not been kind to people who have predicted dates of the Lord's return. Countless attempts have been made, some of them fortified by extensive systems of proof, all to fail when the date predicted fails. In spite of that, this is another attempt at setting the date of the Lord's return. A number of considerations make this, however, an unusual work.

1. Like many preceding predictions, there is a total lack of scholarly agreement with Mr. Camping. In fact, not a reputable scholar in the area of prophecy can be quoted in favor of his position nor a single work supporting it outside of his own writings. If Camping is right, all other Bible students are wrong.

2. Camping's dating system is very unusual because he is an amillenarian, that is, he does not believe that prophecy indicates a literal millennium of Christ's reign on earth after the Second Coming. Ordinarily, amillenarians do not set dates and do not take Scriptures cited for this purpose literally.

3. A curiosity of this development is that some amillenarians are taking the lead in refuting Mr. Camping's books supporting his position.

4. In keeping with his amillennialism, Camping does not interpret the Rapture literally or the events of the Great Tribulation, though he claims we are in the Great Tribulation right now. Obviously, no literal fulfillment of the Book of Revelation is taking place. No reigning world dictator claims to be God and has killed countless individuals who refuse to worship him (Rev. 7:9-14; 20:4-6). There has been no fulfillment of Revelation 6:8, where a fourth of the world is predicted to have been killed when

the fourth seal is broken. The prediction of Revelation 9:14, that a third of the world remaining alive at that time will be killed, has not been fulfilled. The prediction of the seven bowls of the wrath of God in Revelation 16 has not been fulfilled, including the great earthquake which levels the cities of the world in Revelation 16:18-19. The city of Babylon has not been rebuilt and destroyed according to Revelation 18.

5. In a two-hour radio talk show interview with Mr. Camping, he affirmed with absolute certainty that the Lord would come on the date indicated, September 1994. When asked whether he had any substitute suggestion in case it did not happen, he declared he did not. It can be safely predicted that when the date comes and goes, he will come out with an alternate theory, as have most of his predecessors.

6. While many who do not agree with Camping would welcome the coming of the Lord on the date he indicated, the prediction will be subject to lack of fulfillment and disappointment for hundreds who have faithfully followed his teachings and read his books. Though it may turn some to consider their faith in Christ and their dedication to Him, the net result of such false interpretation is extremely detrimental to the study of prophecy which, correctly interpreted, gives the Christian a wonderful hope that the Lord is coming, and perhaps soon.

— John F. Walvoord

Prologue

On September 10, 1992, as listeners gathered around their radios to hear Family Radio's broadcast of "Open Forum," a startling announcement was heard. Harold Camping, weeknight host of the program and president of Family Stations, Inc., declared to his audience that the world would end in just two years!

Beginning with the Apostles, millions of godly people have asked the question, "When will you return, Jesus?" The answer Jesus gave then applies now. In Acts 1:7 the Lord answered, "It is not for you to know times or seasons which the Father has put in His own authority." His Word is the unique and narrow path to truth and safety in these perilous times.

This book will not examine the motives of those who continue to ask the ancient question, "When will Jesus come back the second time?" Rather, this book will examine the definitive answer given by one man who claimed to be 99 percent sure that Christ will come back in September 1994.

This book will also examine the potential harm that may be done to those who follow any teaching that the world will likely end on any given date. In that sense, this book will be valuable until Jesus does come back. For until he comes, teachers and prophets will ignore the clear warnings of Scripture and set dates.

As defined by Noah Webster in his 1828 dictionary, any date-setting scheme is a debacle. Webster defined a debacle as a deluge sweeping the earth, bursting and breaking forth with destructive force. When a man whose voice covers the earth with radio waves says, "Christ has become the enemy of the Church,"[1] this is a debacle. As it was in the days of Noah, so has it become in our day. There is a destructive deluge of delusion and deception sweeping the earth.

On behalf of everyone who has cooperated in publishing this book, I ask those of you who have set your hopes upon a certain date to forgive us for offending you. But if your hopes are dashed by this book, then your faith is misplaced in a false hope. A Christian whose faith and hope are in God will never be disappointed. Invest your faith in a sure hope.

Robert Sungenis, others, and myself have spoken with Harold Camping at length and in person about his teachings which will be examined in this book. We are praying for him and the ongoing ministry of Family Radio. But for the sake of "our common salvation," we have found it necessary to "contend earnestly for the faith which was once for all delivered to the saints" (Jude 3).

Harold Camping's "Open Forum" and "Family Bible Study" are broadcast around the world by the Family Radio network. Family Radio sweeps the earth over short wave in 10 languages. On a daily basis, potentially millions hear Camping's prophetic teachings.

Many others have read Camping's books, *1994?*[2] and *Are You Ready?*[3] Both books are available on cassette for the blind. The 562-page book *1994?* has been translated and published into Spanish, Hindi, Russian, German, Mandarin (Chinese), Portuguese, and Korean.

What is Camping saying and writing that should concern us? Why should you read the book you are now holding? Allow Bob Sungenis, and David Lewis, and myself the privilege to answer those questions for you.

Family Radio is the largest Christian radio network in America, perhaps the most influential in the world. The president of Family Radio would have his listeners and readers believe that in September 1994 (1) the end will come, (2) Jesus will return, (3) all Christians will go to heaven, and (4) the world will be destroyed.

On October 6, 1992, just three weeks after Camping made his announcement and released *1994?* he and I debated his teachings on the WMCA radio program, "Let's Talk, New York." The format was a live two-hour call-in broadcast. This was one of only several times that Camping has defended his teachings publicly outside of "Open Forum."

During this debate I pointed out to Camping that his doctrinal and date-setting conclusions are carefully derived from mathematical calculations. I showed him a numerical error in his book. "I appreciate your sharing that error," Camping said. "We will immediately make correction on that."

Far more serious errors have been made by Camping. One of the most serious is date setting. Robert Cameron, a New Jersey pastor who broadcasts his Sunday service over Family Radio's Newark station, listened to my debate with Camping. He responded to what he heard by printing a Bible study on Mark 13:33: "Take heed, watch and pray; for you do not know when the time is." He compared Mark 13:32-36 with Matthew 24:36-44 and Acts 1:1-7.

Cameron correctly interpreted these Scriptures to mean that God the Father has reserved the knowledge of the timing of the second coming of Christ exclusively for himself.

In his conclusion, Cameron wrote:

> All attempts to discover its timing is prideful, arrogant sin. Additionally, such attempts by persons of prominence serve no useful purpose, and they do cause serious discord in the body of Christ . . . no serious Bible student should ever attempt such date setting.

Harold Camping and his *1994?* book were featured March 8, 1993, on CNN's "Larry King Live" show. Larry King also featured John Noe, author of *The Apocalypse Conspiracy.* When King asked Camping, "On a scale of 1 to 10, how sure are you that Christ is coming in 1994?" Camping responded, "At least 9."

Harold Camping's two date-setting books are long and difficult to read, much less understand. Robert Sungenis has done a marvelous job of simplifying the confusing issues. With remarkable ease and with the insight of an insider, he helps us understand the origins of Camping's divisive doctrines. He is uniquely qualified to be a resource on Camping's errors.

There are three outstanding errors of concern with Camping's doctrine and prophecy. The first is that God has become the enemy of the Church and is destroying it. The second is that Satan uses churches and denominations to kill the citizens of Christ's kingdom. The third is that there is a discoverable timetable for the end of the world.

Destruction of the Church

Camping says in *1994?* "In the Bible we can learn how God plans to destroy the church."[4] He further says, "Satan uses his final opportunity to win a decisive victory over Christ by defeating the external church."[5]

Camping teaches that God has Satan destroy the Church with his blessings! He explains that God's plan is to destroy the Church with false gospel.

For instance, Camping writes that speaking in tongues is the equivalent of eating the forbidden fruit in the Garden of Eden. He teaches that just as God gave the tree of knowledge of good and evil a prominent place in the Garden (Gen. 2:9), God gives tongues prominence in the New Testament. Camping concludes that just as God encouraged Adam to partake of the fruit to bring sin into the world, God encourages many Christians to partake of tongues to bring judgment into the Church.

Regardless of your view of modern speaking in tongues, this method of Bible interpretation must be viewed suspiciously. For Jesus declared He would build His Church victoriously against all the forces of Satan's hell. Clearly, God's unchanging plan is to build, not destroy, His Church (Matt. 16:13-19; Jude 16-21).

Camping writes that "Satan is defeating the true gospel."[6] But surely the "everlasting Gospel" must be eternally victorious and indestructible (Rev. 14:6).

Camping writes that Satan is winning a decisive victory over Christ! This will never be true, not for one moment, not anytime and not anywhere in heaven or on earth.

The Killing of Those Who Follow the True Gospel

The second grievous error to be introduced here is the killing of true believers at the end of the age.

Camping tells us that virtually all congregations teach a false gospel. Therefore Camping exhorts true believers to abandon their church fellowship. They are to leave behind those who think they are worshipping Christ but are in reality serving Satan.

Camping says the true believers are killed by being either driven out or voluntarily leaving their church and denomination. He finds support for this in Revelation 8 and 9. The final Tribulation, as envisioned by Camping, has one-third of everyone in the world's churches and denominations leaving their fellowship to follow the true gospel according to Harold Camping.

Since Camping exhorts not only tithing, but sacrifice, his followers are subtly encouraged to send tithes and sacrificial offerings to Family Radio. Is money an issue here? Consider the following abridged dialogue that took place during my October 6, 1992, debate with Camping and come to your own conclusions:

> Caller: If men leave the church because it is corrupt, if the church is disbanded fundamentally because there will be no more true Church, how will tithes be paid and to whom will tithes be paid?
>
> Camping: When we are driven out of the church, and we ought to try to find another congregation that is still reasonably true, and if we can't find that, we are still to offer our bodies as a living sacrifice as we read in Romans 12 verse 1. Then what we are to do is look around, well, how can I spend my money to give to the Lord as efficiently as possible that the gospel can go out. And I might give it to a tract ministry or I might give it to a radio ministry that is basically sharing the Word of God. We still can make it available to the Lord Jesus Christ even though ideally we ought to try to be still part of a congregation.
>
> Temple: In Mr. Camping's book he says that it is virtually impossible to find a church that is preaching the true gospel. . . . I would like to quote from the "Open Forum" broadcast of October 1, 1992, when a woman listener called and said to Mr. Camping that his book and his predictions have made a big impact on her. She asked the following question, "What about people planning for retirement?" Mr. Camping told the caller to "con-

sider a two year moratorium on putting money away for retirement and make as much money available as possible for the gospel to go out." He then counseled the listener that if Christ had not come by October 1, 1994, that she could "resume preparing for retirement." Mr. Camping in his book includes a chapter, "What is the True Gospel?" There's definitely an inference to exclusivity in his presentation of that so that one would come to the conclusion if one is faithfully following Mr. Camping, that really the only safe place to bring your tithe would be to his ministry.

Camping: Well I think that is an invalid conclusion altogether.

Temple: Any time that a Christian's giving is tied into a date-setting scheme, sir, that is approaching disaster.

Camping: I think everybody's tithing ought to be tied into a prophetic date setting.[7]

Another caller to that same October 1, 1992, broadcast of "Open Forum" asked Camping what happens if he is wrong. "No real damage has been done," was his reply.

Really? No damage? Camping has potentially convinced millions worldwide through Family Radio that the world will end in September 1994. He has told his radio audience to stop saving money, leave their church, and give money to "a radio ministry." Real damage has been done to those who invested faith and finances in him. But the worst damage may be yet to come.

Beyond 1994, lives have been hurt. Christians are being told "there is no time left to trust your pastor or your church."[8] Should they trust Harold Camping? People are being encouraged to leave congregations that do not agree with Camping's unique definition of the true Gospel.

Beyond 1994, multitudes will go into spiritual limbo because they believed Camping and left their church fellowship. People will be spiritually damaged. Camping's teachings must be held up to the searchlight of Scripture. The errors should be publicly refuted and rebuked.

Discoverable Timetable

The third major error of Camping's teaching is that the precise timetable for the end of the world and the second coming of Christ can be discovered.

Camping acknowledges that the Lord's plan of salvation has been available through the various denominations. But, as Camping sees it, the final events of history bring this plan and the Lord's command to evangelize the world to an end.

Based upon his calculation that creation was 13,000 years before 1988, Camping writes, "We therefore should be quite accurate in saying that the New Testament era of sending forth the gospel officially came to an end on May 21, 1988."[9]

Camping does not say that no one could be saved after this date. Rather, he establishes May 21, 1988, as the starting point of Satan's final assault on the Church. Camping teaches that Satan was released from the pit to wreak havoc on the Church from 1988 to 1994.

Counting off 2,300 days from May 21, 1988, brings us to September 6, 1994. Camping says, "When September 6, 1994, arrives, no one else can become saved. The end has come."[10] I say, when September yields to October, may God's grace enable Harold Camping to yield to the Bible's authority and recant this declaration. The alternative could be tragic, as projected in the epilogue of this book.

Incidentally, Camping shared with me personally that he and about 100 followers from his church in California were "forced" to leave his church in 1988 when the pastor and church leaders asked Camping to step down as the adult Sunday school class teacher. I asked Camping if he felt this was a fulfillment of prophecy. He smiled and said that he wouldn't say that, but that it certainly was interesting that this happened just two weeks after May 21, 1988. This new church now has 300 members.[11]

Camping says that Christ cannot return before September 15, 1994. But can any man tell Jesus when He can or cannot come? Christians have been taught to pray, "Jesus come quickly, Jesus come soon!" Yet Camping says Jesus cannot come before the date he has determined.

Jesus said, "It is the wicked and the unprofitable servant who says the Lord delays his coming" (Matt. 24:36-51). Any date-setting scheme is wicked and unprofitable because it declares that the Lord will delay His coming until a time set by a misguided teacher.

Again, according to Camping, the return of Christ cannot be later than September 27, 1994. Camping, like so many before him who were also wrong to set dates, attempts to reconcile his error to Scripture by not declaring the day or the hour of Christ's return. Rather, he is 99 percent, even 99.9 percent, sure that Jesus will return sometime during the last two weeks of September 1994.

Although Camping claims to have reached this date with great care, he cautions that something may have been overlooked that could make his conclusions incorrect. But, since he is 99 percent convinced he is correct, leaving only a 1 percent margin of error, wouldn't this be a more accurate title for his book — *1994!?* That tiny question mark is too small for Camping to hide behind.

Camping's engineered timetable for the end of the world is built on the premise that the world was created exactly 13,000 years before May 21, 1988. That's why God sets aside using churches and denominations to preach the true gospel after that date. Now it appears that Camping would also have his followers understand that Family Radio will stop presenting the gospel after 13,000 days.

During a February 1994 broadcast of "Open Forum," Harold Camping found it interesting to note that if you count off the days from February 4, 1959, when he went to a New York bank and received money to start up Family Radio, until September 6, 1994, it is exactly 13,000 days.

Camping's conclusions become potentially tragic. Family Radio will have been preaching the true gospel for exactly 13,000 days on September 6, 1994. Will Camping no longer offer salvation to Family Radio's audience after that date? When I asked Camping what he will be teaching after September 6, he said that he doesn't expect it to be possible for him to broadcast after then.

Stephen Meyers, a pastor in Pennsylvania, has published several articles refuting the doctrinal errors of Harold Camping. With his permission, I share this letter from a Camping supporter who criticized Meyers for rejecting Camping's ideas. Note the prophetic authority this follower gives Camping because of the 13,000 day announcement.

March 17, 1994
Dear Steve,

Harold Camping's biblical calendar of history shows that the world is exactly 13,000 years old plus 2,300 days for the final Tribulation which will end September 6, 1994. On September 6, 1994, Family Radio will have broadcast the gospel for exactly 13,000 days. This is the likely date for the end of all broadcasting as the world and the universe begin to go into the convulsions which the Lord describes in Matthew 24, Luke 21.

I believe that God has guided the 13,000 days of Family Radio to encourage us that Mr. Camping is certainly correct in his studies and teachings of the biblical calendar and of the end of the world!

If Camping is wrong, then why has God guided the 13,000 days of Family Radio in this way? If Camping is right, and God is guiding this, then you are working against the servant whom God has chosen to share much new understanding about His Word with the world. We'll know soon! God bless you!

The danger is clear for Camping's followers. Not only is Camping caught up in his own unique revelation of prophecy, he also implies that he and Family Radio are a unique end-time fulfillment of God's plan for the redemption of mankind. Cultic leaders always claim to have an exclusive corner on the truth market.

When will we know whether Camping is right or wrong? September 7, 1994? September 28, 1994? No, the student of God's word knows Camping is wrong as soon as he compares his statements to the Bible. Rather than follow man's opinion to "wait and see," the faithful Christian will follow Christ's command to "watch and pray" (Matt. 24:36-51).

Our book is being published to make it clear that Camping's doctrines result from his own private interpretation of the Bible. Camping's prophecies are built upon the sinking sands of time.

This book will also help you see why Camping's doctrines are not only unorthodox, but unscriptural. Dr. Peter Lillback believes this is because Camping views the Scripture as judgment-centered rather than Christ-centered. How else can you explain Camping's alarming statement made in front of me and 1,200 witnesses in Bear, Delaware, on May 14, 1994: "Christ has become the enemy of the Church."

Christians who love God, His Word, and His church, which Christ bought with His own blood, must rise up and say this is wrong. Christ will never become the enemy of His church. He will never hate His own body. The Bible says in Ephesians:

> Christ is the head of the Church; and He is the Saviour of the body . . . Christ also loved the Church and gave himself for it, that He might sanctify and cleanse it with the washing of water by the Word, that He might present it to himself a glorious Church, not having spot or wrinkle or any such thing . . . for no one ever hated his own flesh, but nourishes and cherishes it, just as the Lord does the Church. For we are members of His body (Eph. 5:23-30).

God will forever nourish and cherish every precious member of His own body. Keep yourself in the love of God as you long for the day of His appearing. Keep yourself holy and pure through the blessed hope that is genuine and real.

Christ is coming soon! He may return before you turn the next page. Or He may not return for a very long time.

The blessed hope is guaranteed by the Word of God, not the calendars of men. The Lord Jesus Christ prepares His followers to be long distance runners. But a date-setting teacher prepares his followers to run a sprint. God's Word commands us to "run with endurance the race that is set before us" (Heb. 12:1). But the date setter exhorts his followers to run all-out for the little time he says is left.

What happens when Camping's followers pass his man-made finish line, but the end determined by God is still far ahead? Massive failure. Sprinters do not finish marathons. They run out of steam. They fall down. They drop out. They curse their coach. They are humiliated. They are made to look like fools.

The authors of this book do not want to win an argument. They do not want to win a theological debate. They do not want to win the accolades of men. The authors of this book want you to finish the race that God has set before you. Those who faithfully follow Jesus run with confidence, endure to the end, and finish the course with victory.

May this book be an antidote for the poisonous delusion of date setting. May God's people be released from being held captive by the calendar and made the slaves of dates. May God's children be set free to worship our loving Father "in spirit and truth" (John 4:23).

— Scott Temple

Introduction

In two recently published books, the first, authored with a good measure of ambivalence by the interrogative title *1994?* and the second, with decidedly more assurance in the rhetorical question, *Are You Ready?* Harold Camping, president and founder of Family Stations, Inc., of Oakland, California, has predicted that the end of the world will occur between September 15 and September 27, 1994. Despite disagreement on the dating from his own board and some senior staff,[1] Camping felt that it was a God-given mandate to publish these highly controversial date-setting books.

The November 1992 edition of *Publishers Weekly* noted that *1994?* was the seventh best-selling religious book in America. After just three weeks the book was already being published in the fourth edition. Camping's publishing agent at Vantage Press said that they could not maintain the stock needed to meet the demand. Within a month, she indicated that sales were over 65,000 copies. By early 1993 sales reached 100,000. Sales generated over one million dollars just four weeks after it was released.[2]

Though the easy listening programming of Family Radio portrays a sense of peace and harmony to its audience, behind the scenes Camping has been at odds over doctrine with most of his radio announcers at the Oakland headquarters since the station's inception. Years ago, the managers of the radio stations around the country sought to oust Camping for major doctrinal differences but were unsuccessful. Most were subsequently fired by Camping.

There are definitely two camps at Family Radio headquarters: those who are on Camping's side and those who are not.

Each group keeps a polite distance from the other.

Camping was also at doctrinal odds with the leadership at his own Christian Reformed Church. A few years ago, Camping left the church, taking his many followers with him, and started his own church. The predictions concerning 1994 played a part in the controversy. Until the latter's recent resignation, Camping and his son-in-law, Tom Schaff, were the only elders of the church. For many years they have been without a pastor since they can find no one who agrees with their doctrines.

Considering himself a modern-day Jonah, Camping sincerely believes that his worldwide radio programming and literature are one of the last vestiges of the "true gospel" that can bring anyone to salvation. Jonah was the Old Testament prophet who by *direct command of God,* was told to pronounce God's impending destruction on the Gentile city of Nineveh unless they repented of their wicked deeds within 40 days. The Ninevites did repent, were spared God's judgment, and are highlighted in the New Testament as a great example of faith. Though it is true that Camping is preaching a message of judgment, the analogy with Jonah stops there.

Unlike Jonah, Camping received no direct verbal revelation from God that destruction was coming in a short space of time, i.e., in September 1994. Camping is assuming the role of short-term judgment prophet based strictly on his uncertain and fallible interpretation of the Bible, not on any direct communiqué from God. Second, the Ninevites repented and the city was spared. This is not a possibility in Camping's scenario. Camping believes that most of the world's people will not repent, and even if they do, the world will still end in September 1994. It is my personal opinion that Camping has developed an acute Messiah complex since he believes that only he has the gospel that brings people to salvation and only he knows when the possibility to be saved will be taken away, and that except for him and his followers virtually the whole world is apostate. He likens himself to such biblical characters as Elijah, Jeremiah, Joel, Jehoshaphat, et al. These personalities are chosen since they all portray the image of the faithful prophet standing alone against the apostasy of the people. From this stance Camping makes the bold claim that God has specifically chosen him to be the fulfillment of end-time prophecy and the chief spokesman to the world that Christ will return in September 1994.

Camping claims to have been working on the dating of 1994 for the last 20 years or so. This helps explain why Camping's stations have grown to be the largest Christian network in the world. He has sought a platform from which to disseminate his apocalyptic views, and has finally established the means to propagate this teaching to virtually the whole world. In the early days Camping was already implying that the 1990s would reveal the return of Christ by the consistent refrain, "I do not expect that this world will last till the year 2000." His very early manuscripts from the late 1970s and early 1980s were available for quite a while on the bookshelf at the Family Radio library. In the mid-1980s they were removed from the library since word of Camping's predictions began to leak out to the public. If questions about 1994 continued to arise, Camping would politely dismiss them. Not until the publication of the book *1994?* in September 1992 was the issue publicly reopened by Camping. We wonder that if knowing the date of the end is such an important piece of information, why was it withheld until just two years before the supposed end? More specifically, why was the information about the "tribulation period" withheld from us, which, according to Camping, started May 21, 1988, and was the time when the gospel was silenced so that very few people could receive salvation? If we are in the period of the worst Tribulation the world has ever known because salvation has been taken away, wouldn't it have been prophetically proper to warn us of this awful tragedy *before* it came, rather than after the fact? Did not all of God's prophets with which Camping does not hesitate to equate himself, warn of significant judgments before they came rather than after? Consequently, Camping's prophetic timing seems more like man's doing rather than God's.

Camping believes that the New Testament church, except for a small remnant, has become completely apostate and is ripe for God's judgment. Part of the "true gospel," at least for the wise and enlightened followers, is knowing precisely when Christ will return. In his promotion of the books, Camping has consistently used the 39 radio stations and 109 translator stations owned and operated worldwide by Family Radio. On Family Radio's educational programs, "Open Forum" and "Family Bible Study," Camping promotes his date-setting interpretations as virtually foolproof. Consequently, he bases his everyday decisions, encouraging his followers to do the same, on the fact that the world will not exist after September 1994. Camping states in *1994?:*

> Anyone who decides that he does not believe the fact that the end is so close can do so. But he will be like the proverbial ostrich that sticks his head in the sand. His unbelief will not in any way change the reality of the fact of Christ's return. . . . By God's mercy there are a few months left. However, if this study is accurate, and I believe with all my heart that it is, there will be no extensions in time. There will be no time for second guessing. When September 6, 1994, arrives, no one else can become saved. The end has come.[3]

As noted briefly above, Camping has made a concerted effort to make his views as public as possible — a retreat from the normally low-key ministry he has run for years. Maximum exposure has been achieved by such efforts as appearing on a call-in debate with author John Noe on the popular talk show "Larry King Live," and using a secular publisher for his books where heretofore he has self-published. Presently, Camping dominates the biblical teaching on his 24-hour radio programming which is beamed around the world, both in long and short-wave transmission. His organization is presently distributing hundreds of thousands of gospel tracts, both domestically and abroad, that include the prediction that the world will end in September 1994.

The main tract used by Camping is entitled by the rhetorical question "Does God Love You?" It is Camping's belief that God does not love mankind but actually hates them. According to Camping, God loves only the elect. The tract also includes a reference that the world will end in 1994, and encourages the reader to contact Family Radio for more information. Another tract has been produced by Camping's followers entitled, "Are You Ready: Judgment Day September 1994." Camping allowed this tract to be passed out at his latest debate.

He also fields questions relating to the predictions in his books on his daily talk show, "Open Forum," heard nationally for one and one-half hours, Monday through Friday. His books are presently being translated into many different languages for wide distribution.

Following in the wake of the prophetic debacle in Korea in 1992 in which the prediction that the world would end caused tremendous human tragedy in its aftermath, Camping is presently having his apocalyptic books published in Korean for wide distribution in that country. Not every publisher has accepted Camping's book, however. Though his book *1994?* had been translated into Russian, Alexander Semchenko, who operates the largest publishing house in Russia, decided not to publish the book.

He has also appeared in three debates, the first against Scott Temple on WMCA in New York in 1992; the second against John F. Walvoord, chancellor of Dallas Theological Seminary on KFAX in San Francisco in January 1994; and finally in May 1994 against Dr. Tremper Longman III, professor of Old Testament at Westminster Theological Seminary and Dr. Peter Lillback, a Presbyterian pastor.

Camping was originally asked to debate R.C. Sproul and James Montgomery Boice, but he declined in favor of Longman and Lillback. I had also asked Camping for a debate in April 1993, but he declined in a letter to me, saying, "I have neither the time nor the interest in a public debate."

Camping also encourages his listening audience to write to the producers of popular talk shows like Oprah Winfrey, Phil Donahue, and the like, so that he can be invited to be a guest to promote the date of September 1994. It is apparent from all this publicity that it is Camping's intention to disseminate his views worldwide.

As a former employee of Harold Camping, I write the main body of this critique as one who knows quite well the unique methodology that led him to this very controversial prediction. After graduating from seminary,[4] I took a position as a Bible instructor at the newly formed Family Radio School of the Bible in 1982. Things were going well until I began to question some of the doctrines that were being taught by Camping. At the end of my second year, these disagreements led to my release from the school. Instructors before and after me found themselves in the same situation as they quickly became a statistic in the high turnover rate among Family Radio employees. The erroneous interpretations I discovered during my work at Family Radio persist to this day and permeate the books *1994?* and *Are You Ready?* Since the mere titles of the two books have created undo alarm for many unsuspecting Christians who have neither the time nor acumen to digest the combined 1,000 pages of material, I feel an obligation to show from the inside, a brief yet thorough critique of Camping's theories and his self-appointed mission. It is our hope that *all* those who have felt some measure of anxiety on hearing or reading of *1994?* or *Are You Ready?* but didn't quite know how to refute its complicated and intimidating analysis, will receive a large measure of relief upon reading this critique.

In brief, the main point that this critique will levy is that though Camping claims that numerical theories that purport to chart the end of the world must be supported by the Bible[5], it is precisely this premise that Camping continually violates in his books. The Bible simply does not explicitly teach any of the numerological theories of Harold Camping.

The chapter headings of this book have not been chosen to disparage Harold Camping in any way, but to alert the reader to the major categories of error that have led to his controversial prediction. Among those in the past who have set dates for the end of the world, a pessimistic view of the Church and the world occupies much of the theorizing as well as the use of peculiar and exclusive forms of biblical exegesis. The various chapters of this book highlight these tendencies among apocalyptic date setters.

For example, William Miller, founder of the Adventists (later known as Seventh Day Adventists), who predicted that the world would end in 1843, shows a remarkable similarity in exegetical style to Harold Camping. Miller, using only the Bible and a concordance as his sources, used the 2,300 evenings and mornings of Daniel 8:14 to arrive at his dating.

Miller, like Camping, also thought that the "sanctuary" of Daniel 8:14 represented the New Testament church that had become apostate and would be cleansed at Christ's second coming. When Christ's second coming did not occur, many left the movement. Miller then set a second date in 1844 based on a meticulous study of Old Testament types. Many followers sold their goods and made daily plans based on Miller's prediction. When the second date did not occur, many Millerites went back to their former denomination or abandoned Christianity altogether.[6]

Actually, even many of Camping's followers with whom I have talked have not read his books or do not understand the intricate calculations Camping presents, yet they believe his predictions because they trust him. I have painstakingly analyzed and researched his calculations down to the very decimal. Though I cannot, for lack of time and space, write on all of the calculations in his two books, I have tried to make a detailed analysis of most of the salient numerological theories and theological points of the books, while making general comments on issues and calculations that are not as prominent. However, once one becomes familiar with the basic exegetical framework from which Camping is operating, almost all of his theories and calculations can be understood within about three or four basic categories. Some of my analysis will overlap, yet each chapter will show a different angle from which to view and critique Camping's work.

Since after 30 years of programming and literature Camping has attained such a high degree of notoriety, and since we are very near the presumed dates of September 15-27, 1994, it is incumbent upon those who have any interest at all about the goings-on in the Christian world to take stock of Camping's prediction and find a satisfactory answer, either pro or con, to his claims.

Contrary to some other critics, I do not believe Camping is a fringe nut-case who has nothing better to do than put his ministry on the line by making outlandish predictions. He actually believes he is doing what is best for his fellow man. For the most part, Camping is very orthodox in his theological views, believing in, for example, the deity of Christ, the existence of hell, salvation by grace, and many other traditional doctrines. From my personal experience with Camping, he is a very intelligent and thoughtful person. He is a moral and upstanding citizen and tries his best to put God first in his life. He lives a very modest lifestyle, not being flamboyant or self-indulgent in the least. Hence, we do not wish in this book to attack Harold Camping personally but only to critique his apocalyptic views in the fairest and most erudite manner.

As ironic as it may seem, we hope that Christ will return in September 1994. The sooner the world ends the better. True Christians have learned to loathe their life on earth knowing that a far better life exists with God in heaven. Contrary to what he says of his critics, we do not deny that September 1994 could be the end of the world, as Camping claims, because we "refuse to accept the truth of the Bible," rather, after a thorough analysis of his methods and theories, we do not think Camping has interpreted the Bible correctly. It is as simple as that. As one will witness in the remainder of this critique, because his exegesis of the Bible concerning the timing of the end can be shown to be so convoluted, if, perchance, Christ returns in 1994, I believe it will be in spite of Harold Camping's interpretations, not because of them.

Finally, to those readers who, because of Harold Camping's teaching, believe the world will end in September 1994, please read carefully, thoughtfully, and with an open mind, the remainder of this critique. Try to put your opinions and persuasions aside for the moment and give this book a fair and objective hearing. To help in doing so, remember the wise words of Solomon:

> The first to present his case seems right, till another comes forward and questions him (Prov. 18:17).

In this critique, I have included where one can find the matter under discussion by referencing the page numbers of *1994?* or *Are You Ready?* in parentheses. Pages from *Are You Ready?* are preceded by AYR.

It should be noted that the other authors of this book, Scott Temple and David Allen Lewis, hold to the premillennial view of eschatology. Though I admire many tenets of the premillennial view, I neither make specific support nor denounce it in this book. At present, I do not embrace any particular view but I am thoroughly familiar with the gamut of eschatological perspectives.

— Robert Sungenis

1

Camping Separates Himself from Previous End-Time Date Setters

by Robert Sungenis

Unlike the many date setters that came before him, Camping tries his best to assure his readers that his prediction has the highest degree of probability since he has based his calculations strictly on the numbers of the Bible; not on the changing and uncertain political, social, or cataclysmic events of the world as his predecessors have done. Though it is true that many end-time predictors have used world events to coincide with biblical prophecies, it is a fact that a significant proportion have depended almost exclusively on the numbers of the Bible to predict the return of Christ. One of the latest of these numerologists was Edgar C. Whisenant who predicted that the Rapture would occur on September 11-13, 1988.[1] When the Rapture did not occur, Whisenant quickly discovered his supposed error, recalculated his figures, and changed the year to 1989. Of course, that date was wrong, too. Like Camping, Whisenant claimed special God-given knowledge of such things as the dating of the seventieth week of Daniel, a correspondence between Old Testament feasts and eschatological events, and a precise understanding of the symbolic use of numbers in the Bible.

Second, as much as he attempts to separate himself from other date setters, it is not true that Camping has totally abandoned the use of political or social events as an integral part of his theory. Like Whisenant before him, one of the major working premises in Camping's analysis is the re-establishment of the nation of Israel in 1948. Camping has written at length on this subject,[2] claiming that the biblical references to the *"fig tree in leaf"* refer to the national regathering of Israel in Palestine (p. 437). Then, by a simple addition of 40 years to this date (40 years supposedly being God's testing time for Israel to turn to Christ), Camping proposes that the prelude to the end of the world began precisely on May 21, 1988. Israel's 40 year rejection of Christ, along with the general apostasy of the Gentile churches throughout the world, ushers in the 6.4 year "tribulation period" of God's judgment on Israel and the Church. This period of judgment will end with the final judgment in September 1994.

One major problem with Camping's view of modern-day Israel is that the Bible never explicitly says that Israel, then or now, is represented by a fig tree. There are certainly usages of the fig tree in parabolic contexts, even as other types of trees are used symbolically in the Bible, but there is no definitive typecast of the fig tree to the nation of Israel in either the Old or New Testament. Camping is reading into the references to the fig tree that which coincides with his end-time theory, i.e., that Israel will come under God's judgment again, as opposed to past God-directed judgments by the Assyrians, Babylonians, and the Romans in their respective eras, because as a nation they have denied Christ as their Saviour. The fig tree without fruit, only leaves, is, according to Camping, symbolic of the current unbelief in modern-day Israel. Camping attempts to support this view by appealing to Mark 11:14 in which Jesus curses a fig tree so that it never bears fruit, as well as Luke 13:6 concerning the parable of the man who, not finding any figs on his tree, decides to fertilize it and wait one more year for fruit before he cuts it down. Camping claims that the three years the man does not find any figs represents three different epochs in Israel's history, namely, 1) the Assyrian captivity, 2) the Babylonian captivity, and 3) the demise of national Israel in the first century A.D. The fourth year the man returns for figs represents when Israel became a nation in 1948 wherein God is once again looking for fruit, i.e., saving faith in Christ. This will not be the only time Camping turns mere parables into significant prophetic statements in his books. This conclusion is certainly contrived, since the Bible gives no such interpretation to this parable. In context, Jesus is merely attempting to teach general truths about repentance. For example, in Luke 13:1-8 Jesus is explaining to the people who were concerned about the sufferings of the Galileans and those in the tower of Siloam that regardless of who you think you are, if you do not repent in a certain space of time, God will likewise punish you. In this way, Jesus is teaching that each of us is like a fig tree that must bear the fruit of repentance or soon be cut down by God. In Mark 11:12-26, the only lesson that Jesus draws from the cursed fig tree is to teach the Apostles about faith. As Peter marvels the next day that the fig tree is withered, Jesus reminds them that they also can obtain such great faith to do great works, even to the point of casting a mountain into the sea. Why is this lesson taught at this particular time? Because soon the Apostles' faith will be severely tested as Jesus is arrested and sent to be crucified (Luke 22:31). In other passages, the fig tree, as well as *all* other trees, are used only as an object lesson for people to be aware of what is going on in the world, not as a forecast for national Israel (Luke 21:29-31). The majority of Jewish people have disbelieved in Christ for two millennia and thus it is no surprise that they are in unbelief as a nation today. Further, Camping is not consistent to his own spiritualization. He claims that the fig tree in Revelation 6:13 represents the apostate corporate Church, not national Israel. Such mixing and matching of symbols occurs frequently in his two books.

Camping also makes passing reference to such sociological crises as the AIDS epidemic among homosexuals, purporting that it is a dramatic sign that God is beginning to increase his wrath on the sins of mankind as a prelude to judgment day. Camping cites Romans 1:27b ("and received in themselves the due punishment for their perversion") and claims that it is a *prophecy* that AIDS will occur in the tribulation period. Camping states: "The language of Romans 1 . . . especially applies to the final

Tribulation period . . . a homosexual runs a great risk of receiving the AIDS virus: the prophecy of Romans 1 comes alive." (p. 210-211). Though AIDS, like any other disease, could be a judgment from God, it cannot be said that Romans 1 is making a specific prophecy concerning AIDS occurring during the Tribulation period. First, the verbs used in Romans 1:27 are Greek present participles. This means that Paul was writing about instances of this judgment that were occurring in his time. It is something God has always done and always will do. He judges sin where and when he sees it. Second, AIDS did not start in Camping's Tribulation period of May 1988. AIDS occurred in the homosexual community approximately a decade prior. Third, it must be acknowledged that AIDS, like any other disease, could simply be a product of the germ-infested world we live in. Because AIDS infects and devastates the heterosexual (adult and child), IV drug users, and hemophiliacs with bad blood transfusions, it is not solely a homosexual phenomenon. At present AIDS kills only a fraction of the world's people as compared to cancer and heart disease which account for approximately 75 percent of the mortality in the world. We could view the contracting of AIDS in non-homosexual groups as merely the fallout of homosexual sin. However, we would have to acknowledge that the apparent rise and tolerance of homosexual behavior is suspiciously similar to the prevalence of homosexuality in other past cultures on the brink of destruction, e.g., Sodom and Gomorrah, or the Greek and Roman Empires which actually institutionalized homosexuality. Consequently, if Christ were to base His second coming on the deteriorated moral condition of the world, considering the prevalence of such present social ills as homosexuality, abortion, sexual promiscuity, divorce, adultery, murder, etc., our day can be considered a worthy candidate for God's judgment. By the same token, however, God could administer this judgment in 1995 or 2045 or any other date, not necessarily September 1994. Sin in its worst forms, even homosexuality, has been with us since the dawn of man. Though the prevalence of sin keeps us alert for God's judgment, it cannot be used as a biblical criterion to chart a specific date for the end of the world.

2

Neutralizing Jesus' Statement Concerning Not Knowing the Day or Hour of His Return

by Robert Sungenis

One remarkable similarity between Whisenant and Camping is the concerted effort each makes to alter the clear language of Mark 13:32 or Matthew 24:36 which state: "But of that day and that hour knoweth no man, no, not the angels of heaven, neither the Son, but the Father." Since this verse must obviously be answered before proceeding with their predictions, one will notice various exegetical contortions in which they engage to reach this point. Whisenant gives a long dissertation on the differences between the Greek words for "know," claiming that the gospel writer chose a word that denotes *intuitive* knowledge rather than *certain* knowledge, which supposedly allows him to calculate, with certainty, the exact day of Christ's return.

Camping's dealing with Mark 13:32 is much more creative than Whisenant's. He has a two-pronged explanation. Using the spiritualizing method of interpretation that saturates most of his exegesis of the Bible, Camping proposes that the knowledge of the Son is not necessarily speaking of a *chronological* day and hour, rather, of the Father's *judgment* upon the Son at the crucifixion. Hence, the Son did not *"know"* the day or hour since He had not gone to the Cross as yet when He spoke the words of Mark 13:32. Camping supports this novel exegesis by doing a word study on how the Bible uses the phrase *day and hour*. Since the phrase is sometimes used in contexts of God's judgment, Camping gives himself license to spiritualize the phrase making it refer to the "experience of judgment" (p. 316). The verse is also said to be applicable to mankind since they have not "experienced" God's final judgment either and thus do not know the *day or hour*.

What Camping fails to recognize is that Mark 13:33, (which, curiously, is not referenced at all in *1994?* as opposed to Mark 13:32 which is quoted over a dozen times) clarifies the chronological meaning of the *day and hour* used in Mark 13:32 by the addition of: *"for you do not know when the time is."* The English word *"time"* is from the Greek word *"kairos"* which refers to chronological time, never to experience. In addition, such phrases as, *"My Lord delays his coming,"* and *"in a day he looks not for him . . . and in an hour he is not aware"* in Matthew 24:48-50, and *"at evening, or at midnight . . . or in the morning"* in Mark 13:35, clearly point to time and time categories, not experience. Jesus certainly knew when He was going to the Cross and thus to mix and match time with experience as Camping does has no biblical validity.

Once he neutralizes the literal meaning of Mark 13:32, Camping feels he has the prerogative to begin calculating the day of Christ's return. However, Camping is well aware what a bold assertion he is making in predicting the date of the end of the world, and he also knows that many worthy critics reject his spiritualized interpretations of the Bible. Hence, to make his date setting more palatable, Camping has adopted a second interpretation of Mark 13:32, totally different than the first. He states that if one insists on taking Jesus' words literally, then no one, not even Jesus, can know the day and the hour of His return, then he (Camping) is not being unbiblical since he has not predicted the *precise* day and hour of Christ's return but any one of 13 days. This is so because Camping claims that Christ will return between September 15 and September 27, 1994 (p. 525, 531).

These two diametrically opposed interpretations of the *day and hour* of Mark 13:32 are a prime example of the exegetical duplicity that is found in much of Camping's interpretive efforts. Even some of Camping's supporters try to defend this duplicity without admitting the slightest tinge of inconsistency.[1] There is constant switching between different forms of interpretation depending on whichever approach fits the theological agenda at hand. As I will show in more detail later, in many cases Camping first forms the doctrine he desires and then makes the Scripture conform to his belief by twisting the passage with spiritualized interpretations. *1994?* and *Are You Ready?* are constant victims of this tendency.

In addition, Mark's Gospel curtails knowing even the month and the year in the phrasing, "You do not know the time." As noted above, "time" is from the Greek "kairos" which refers to any time period. Hence, Mark prohibits knowing the hour, day, month, year, or even century.

One obvious refutation to Camping's *"experience"* theory is that if Camping were to be consistent to his own definition this would mean that God the Father, since He is the only one who *knows* the day and hour, would have had to *experience* judgment of some kind. This follows logically from Camping's self-imposed definition of the word "know" and consequently shows a glaring inconsistency in his approach since it is obvious that the Father has never experienced judgment of any kind. Camping answers this anomaly by a slight modification in the parameters of his definition, namely, that the judgment of Mark 13:32 refers to the fact that "no one who *is* to experience Judgment Day has yet experienced Judgment Day" (p. 318) [emphasis mine]. Since the Father was not scheduled to be judged, then the spiritual meaning of Mark 13:32 does not apply to Him. This certainly seems to be a convenient way of modifying one's premise to fit one's biased understanding of the passage.

If Camping's claim is correct that Jesus totally retained His divine omniscience when He was a man and therefore knew the exact day and hour of His coming when He made the statement in Mark 13:32, then by the same omniscience He should also have known what it would be like to experience judgment. Moreover, if the Father, being omniscient, knew what the experience of judgment would be like, then certainly the Son, also being omniscient, would know what the experience of judgment would be like. There is no limitation to what one knows when one is omnisicient. Therefore, Camping's contention that the Son can know the day and hour of His coming but not know what judgment would be like, is totally invalid. He cannot claim that Christ, being omniscient, can know one thing but not another. Hence, we must maintain the biblical truth, however difficult it may seem on the surface, that there are some things known by the Father that are not known by the Son. Jesus confirms this in Acts 1:7 as He reinforces the principle of Mark 13:32 by specifiying that the *Father* alone has set times and dates by His own authority. Apparently there is a division of labor and responsibility in the Godhead based on the authority invested in each divine person. The Father is in control of when events will occur — the Son is not.

Regarding the second interpretation that Camping assigns to Mark 13:32 (that he is not predicting the exact day of Christ's return, but only the month and year), it must be recognized that it would be pointless for Jesus to make a distinction between knowing the day of His coming as opposed to knowing only the month and year of His coming. What possible reason could there be to let us know the month and the year but not the day? Since the month can at most be only 31 days from the actual day of Christ's return, there is virtually no difference in time between the month and the day, especially since the world has existed for thousands of years. Knowing the month of Christ's return would certainly carry the same message of His imminent return to the individual as knowing the day, and thus there would be no useful purpose for Jesus to make a distinction between the two. As a result, Camping's alternative interpretation of Mark 13:32 not only twists Jesus' words, but it makes no practical sense.

Though he has posed possible calculations to determine the exact day of Christ's return, Camping does this only to demonstrate that it is virtually impossible to be certain of the exact date. To support this view, Camping claims that God has deliberately put confusing information in the Bible so we cannot know the exact day but overwhelming information so that we can know the month and year. It is my opinion that Camping promotes such observations in order to placate those who feel he is wrong in even predicting the month and year.

The phrase *day and hour* should not be stretched to the point that it distorts Jesus' simple intention of expressing the general truth that He will come when not expected. Whether literal, figurative, or idiomatic, Jesus' words convey this clear and unrelenting truth. The words "hour" or "day," singly or in combination, are often used in idiomatic Greek to express a general time or season (John 2:4; 5:35; 16:2,32; 1 Cor. 15:30; Philem. 15; 1 John 2:18; Luke 6:23; 19:42). On the other hand, often when the Gospel writers wanted to specify a certain time frame they would use an appropriate modifier, such as "the third hour" (Matt. 26:40; Mark 15:25; John 11:9). Reading Matthew 24:36 in its plain sense, the sensitive reader leaves with the impression that Jesus is saying that He could come back at anytime and hence one must keep his life in order without slacking. Jesus' most pressing desire was for His followers to *continue* in obedience and virtue. By using *day and hour* Jesus is not secretly implying that He is creating a porthole through which to calculate the month and year of His return, rather, He is desiring that His servants do not become lax in their waiting for Him and fall into temptation (Matt. 24:48). The only thought in Jesus' mind is the preservation of one's salvation, not the exact timing of the end. This intention is confirmed by the three pericopes He gives immediately following the Olivet discourse — the 10 virgins, the talents, and the judgment of the nations (Matt. 25). Each story concludes with the fact that some were obedient and thus ready for their master's return, while some were disobedient and not ready. None are concerned with trying to find out *when* the Master will return.

We should also add that the Old Testament examples of judgment that Jesus uses to give the overall sense of His meaning in the Olivet discourse do not suggest that one can know the month and the year of His coming. For example, Jesus remarks that in the days of Noah the people were marrying and giving in marriage until the day that Noah entered the ark (Matt. 24:37-39). It is apparent from the Genesis account that Noah did not know the exact timing of the end until seven days before he entered the ark (Gen. 7:1-4). Before this, Noah could not pinpoint the specific month, day, or hour that the Lord's judgment would come. He may have been able to know the year *if* the meaning of Genesis 6:3 is that there were to be 120 years to the Flood. Even then, Noah would have known the *year* of the Flood because God *verbally* told him so. Camping claims to know something about the end of time from merely reading the Bible that even Noah didn't know by divine revelation till seven days before the Flood. Similarly, Lot was warned of the impending destruction of Sodom and Gomorrah only one day before the judgment came (Luke 17:28-30). Though Abraham was warned that Sodom and Gomorrah would probably be destroyed, he was not given a precise timetable as to if and when it would occur (Gen. 18:32-33). This is the sense of His coming that Jesus portrays in the Synoptic Gospels — a sudden, almost instantaneous event whose exact timing no one knows (Luke 17:34-36). In fact, Jesus indicates that there will be some Christians who think they know when He is coming but He will come at a time they have not thought of: "Therefore *you* also be ready: because an hour which *you* do not think of, the Son of Man comes" (Matt. 24:44).

Most scholars understand that the reason Jesus did not know the day and hour of His return is due to the mystery of the hypostatic union — the interplay between the divine and human natures of Jesus. In being both God and man, Jesus is totally unique. There are qualities about Him that we will never comprehend just as we will never comprehend the nature of the Trinity. Nevertheless, it is a fact drawn from the Scriptures that Jesus did not use the powers and prerogatives of His divine nature unless it was necessary to accomplish His work of redemption. When Jesus went about His daily life He did not usually avail himself of His divine omniscience and omnipotence unless the moment demanded it. Philippians 2:6-8 specifies that Jesus "emptied himself" to become a man. Hebrews 5:7 indicates that Jesus "learned" obedience. Even though Jesus was God, there were certain self-imposed limitations to His divine nature while He was on earth. Perhaps Jesus learned the day and hour of His return when He ascended to the Father, but did not know it when He was on earth prior to His death.

3

Inventing One's Own Criterion for Correct Biblical Chronology

by Robert Sungenis

In reading the over 1,000 combined pages of *1994?* and *Are You Ready?* if one has been listening to Harold Camping's ministry over the years it is not hard to see that his life's work has been put into these two books. The same themes that he has been teaching for the past 30 years at Family Radio have culminated in these voluminous works. For example, pivoting off of earlier work,[1] Camping claims to have cracked the code for the genealogies of Genesis 5 and 11, proposing that the date of creation is 11,013 B.C. Starting from Edwin Thiele's date of 931 B.C. for the division of the monarchy,[2] Camping works his way back through the period of the Judges, the Egyptian sojourn, and the Genesis genealogies to arrive at 11,013 B.C. for the creation of Adam. The significance of 11,013 is reinforced by Camping as he alerts us to the fact that if one adds 13,000 years to 11,013 he will arrive at 1988 A.D., which according to Camping, is the beginning of the "final Tribulation period" and the six-year prelude to the return of Christ. The number 13 features prominently in Camping's end-time forecasting since he claims it is a highly significant symbolic number.

There is an undercurrent that Camping creates throughout *1994?* and *Are Your Ready?* that he is the first one in all of history to correctly understand biblical chronology, thus he touts his theories as the only viable solution. It is a fact, however, that many aspects of his genealogical "discoveries" have been known for quite some time, e.g., that the genealogies of Genesis 5 and 11 are not necessarily father/son relationships. Either Camping is unaware of these past developments or deliberately avoids referencing them.

It is interesting to note that Camping repeatedly tells his followers to trust only in the Bible rather than books written by other theologians. The irony in this statement is that Camping has written over a dozen books giving his unique interpretation of the Bible that he strongly encourages people to read and study to know the truth. Hence, one is not supposed to read the books of other theologians, even though they quote consistently from the Bible, but it is quite all right to read Camping's books. Apparently, Camping feels that one cannot glean from the Scripture what he has learned of the world's demise unless they are guided by his books. Since Camping feels he is the only one who has been blessed by God with end-time truth, then a conclusion like this makes perfect sense to him.

One of the major unproven assumptions that Camping makes in his genealogical theory is that the individuals in the genealogies who were not father/son relations would of necessity be the calendar reference patriarch for their entire lifetime (p. 288). Though this is possible it is by no means certain. Camping attempts to prove his patriarch theory by focusing on the time spans of Levi, Kohath, Amram, and Aaron saying that if added correctly they will give the sum of exactly 430 years — the time, according to Exodus 12:40, that the Israelites were in Egypt. But in arriving at the total of 430 years for these four individuals Camping must assume that: 1) Jacob spent 40 years in Haran instead of 20, and 2) that Levi was 21 years older than Joseph. This information is crucial to Camping's theory but it is by no means provable from the Bible. Also, Camping cannot prove that the time spans from Levi to Aaron can be used as a model for the genealogies in Genesis 5 and 11.

Camping does not hesitate to castigate the work of other chronologists who have not arrived at the same scheme of Old Testament dating that he has. Though Camping is certainly more faithful to the Bible than many liberal commentators who invariably disregard the biblical evidence in favor of pet archeological and theological theories, he has his own problems to deal with. For example, Camping faults the work of Edwin Thiele because Thiele adds 12 years to the reign of Hoshea. Thiele claimed that Hoshea's reign cannot be reconciled any other way with the remaining biblical data, and thus, there must have been a scribal error in recording Hoshea's dates, an error caused by the confusion and disruption of Jewish society by the attack from Assyria in the eighth century B.C. Camping does his best to patch up Thiele's work, but ends up creating his own anomalies and apparent fudging of biblical numbers.

After a very analytical and precise recounting of the reigns of the kings of Judah, Camping realizes that there is one biblical reference that even he can't reconcile. The verse is 2 Chronicles 22:2 which in the Masoretic text states that Ahaziah was 42 years old when he began to reign over Judah. This is in direct contradiction to 2 Kings 8:26 which states that Ahaziah was 22 years old when he began to reign. Rather than see a scribal error as Thiele did with Hoshea, Camping resorts to saying that God must have had a "spiritual" reason for recording the number 42 in 2 Chronicles 22:2 (AYR: p. 165). In claiming a "spiritual" reason, Camping thinks that he has gotten himself off the hook but he has inadvertently opened Pandora's box. For one who prides himself on preserving the historical accuracy of the Scripture when he engages in spiritualization, Camping does not do so here. Effectively, Camping is claiming that God allowed an historical error into the biblical record because He deemed the spiritual truth of 42 years, (which spiritual truth Camping does not explain for us), more important than the historical truth, at least for the chronicler as opposed to the author of Kings. Camping is in far more dangerous territory in making this claim than Thiele is for claiming a simple scribal error. Camping has done exactly what he has consistently accused others of doing — denying the historical accuracy of the Scripture in favor of an overriding spiritual presupposition. As we will see later, this is a prime example of the paramount importance Camping places on spiritualizing the biblical text. It can even supersede the historical facts.

One interesting interpretive idiosyncrasy that leads Camping to *force* various numbers of Scripture is that he does not believe there can be any scribal errors in the transmission of the biblical text, that is, manuscript copying done *after* the original autographs were written. He believes God preserved the copying of the biblical text down through the centuries such that versions like the King James Bible were translated from completely error-free Greek manuscripts. This shows a very naive understanding about the history of biblical transmission. There are, for example, over 5,000 Greek manuscripts of the New Testament, most showing various discrepancies, some large and some small, between one another. Similarly, the Hebrew and other Semitic versions also have numerous discrepancies. The Bible does not specify that the transmission of the text was inspired, only the original writing of the text was inspired, which unfortunately does not exist any longer.

Another text that Camping admits he cannot understand is 1 Samuel 13:1 which in the Masoretic text literally reads from the Hebrew: "A son of one year was Saul when he became king and for two years he ruled as king over Israel." This would mean that Saul died when he was three years old. The Septuagint says that Saul was "thirty years old when he became king and reigned for forty-two years." This latter number is recorded in Acts 13:21 as "forty years." In many instances the Septuagint helps us to reconstruct the original text since, as confirmed by the Dead Sea Scrolls, it was also a translation of a Hebrew text.

Irrespective of these facts, since the writing of *Are You Ready?* Camping has withdrawn the spiritual interpretation of 2 Chronicles 22:2 saying now that the 42 years of Ahaziah is historically correct ("Family Bible Study," April 4, 1994). Perhaps he realized the implications of implying that God put an historical error in the Bible for spiritual reasons. To make these numbers fit, Camping says that though Ahaziah was 22 years old when he began to reign, the reference to being 42 years old in 2 Chronicles 22:2 refers not to Ahaziah's reign but to the 42-year span from the beginning of Omri's reign in 884 B.C. to the first year of Ahaziah's reign in 842 B.C. Camping allows himself to go back to Omri's reign to begin the 42 years, because he claims the Hebrew word "ben" used in 2 Chronicles 22:2 does not necessarily refer to an immediate son of a father but to a future descendent. However, this is still a distortion of the Hebrew text since the same exact Hebrew grammatical phrasing is used in 2 Kings 8:26 which refers to Ahaziah's chronological age of 22, not the time span from one descendent to another.

It should also be noted that though Camping seems to have an airtight analysis of the complicated reigns of the kings of Israel and Judah, he does so only by assuming the existence of numerous *"coregencies,"* i.e., that two kings reigned simultaneously for a period of time. Though coregencies are certainly possible, we become somewhat suspicious of Camping's chronology when we discover that he has included a coregency in his calculations with almost every other king. There are no less than a dozen coregencies claimed by Camping in his chronological scenario. Some of these coregencies last over 20 years, a bit long by anyone's standards (AYR: p. 139-174). Claiming a coregency for two kings, whose biblical dates would otherwise be hard to reconcile, is very convenient. If one can't make the numbers fit he can just slide them up or down the chronological scale and call the overlap a "coregency." But an inordinate amount of coregencies casts much doubt on Camping's proposed solution, especially in light of the fact that he is using this solution to help arrive at 1994 for the return of Christ, something Edwin Thiele did not dare to do.

There are other anomalies in the biblical record to which Camping gives a quick answer without realizing the implications of his solution for the rest of the Bible. For example, it is recorded in 2 Chronicles 16:1 that in the thirty-sixth year of the reign of Asa king of Judah, Baasha, king of Israel, attacked Asa. This presents a difficulty for Camping since he holds that the last year of Baasha's reign was 886 B.C., while the thirty-sixth year of Asa's reign was 875 B.C. This 11-year difference would make Baasha's reign cease before he attacked Asa. Camping attempts to solve this problem by saying that the reference to the "thirty-sixth year of Asa" is not starting from the beginning of

Asa's reign but from Rehoboam's reign (AYR: p. 133-135). This again is a convenient way of avoiding the difficulty. The logical question that surfaces here is why the chronicler said Asa when he meant Rehoboam, or, why did he record 36 years when he meant some other amount of years? Further suspicions are cast on this solution since there is no other king for which Camping claims such a transposition. It is conveniently chosen in this instance because it helps Camping's chronology pan out. At the same time, however, Camping has inadvertently accused the Scripture of being imprecise with its references to which king is reigning at a specific time.

4

Validating One's Theories by Producing Numbers with Multiple Zeros

by Robert Sungenis

Irrespective of whether his Old Testament dating is correct, one thing that is immediately obvious throughout the numerical equations of *1994?* and *Are You Ready?* is that Camping is fascinated by large whole numbers which include many zeros. Perhaps due to his background with large numbers as a civil engineer, Camping has convinced himself that because he can bridge gaps in biblical time by numbers with many zeros, he feels he has found the ultimate criterion for establishing precise biblical chronology. This premise is the backbone of *1994?* and *Are You Ready?* since most of the calculations that Camping uses to arrive at 1994 are implicitly validated by the fact that the sum contains several zeros. The naive reader is impressed by these large whole numbers and thus they become one of the main sources of attraction to Camping's end-time theory. But for one such as Camping, who doggedly claims that one's method of interpretation must first be validated by the Bible (p. 382), it remains a fact that the Bible nowhere gives validation to use zero-filled numbers as criteria to prove its chronological framework. Though Camping depends on multiple zeros and large, evenly divisible numbers to validate his theories, the largest time bridge that the Bible offers is the 480 years of 1 Kings 6:1 or the 430 years of Exodus 12:40, or possibly the 70 weeks of Daniel 9:24.

One of Camping's more popular numbers is 2,000. By a simple addition of 2,000 years to his presumed date of 7 B.C. for the birth of Christ, Camping shows how easy it is to arrive at A.D. 1994 (7 B.C. + 2000 = A.D. 1994, subtracting one year to compensate for no year "zero"). Camping also reminds us that there were 2,000 years between the presumed date of Jacob's birth in 2007 B.C. and the birth of Christ in 7 B.C. That the number 2,000 could be used as a criterion for determining correct biblical chronology is based on Camping's symbolism that the number 2 represents the Church or the witness of the gospel. Hence, the time from Christ's first coming in 7 B.C. to his second coming in A.D. 1994 is a 2,000 year span in which "the witness of the gospel is being spread by the church." For further evidence, Camping postulates that if this bi-millennium had started at A.D. 33 (instead of 7 B.C.), which, according to Camping was the year of the crucifixion, then 2,000 years later, A.D. 2033, would immediately become a candidate for the return of Christ. Yet the possibility of Christ returning in A.D. 2033 is discounted by another numerological theory of Camping's concerning the 2,000 swine of Mark 5:13 and the 200 cubits of John 21:8. Spiritualizing the 2,000 swine or 200 cubits as representing the time between Pentecost and the point the last person on earth is saved, Camping theorizes that the specific phrasing, "*about* two thousand swine" and "*about* two hundred cubits," respectively, will not allow an exact counting of 2,000 years between A.D. 33 and A.D. 2033. Hence, the 2,000 year period can be "extended" beyond A.D. 33 to other important gospel landmarks, most notably, 7 B.C. when Christ was supposedly born. Hence, the "prophecy" of the parable containing the word "about" is fulfilled since there are 2,039 years between 7 B.C. and A.D. 2033. In this instance, the inexact numbers from two remote New Testament narratives that Camping has magically turned into "prophecies" become a major criterion for judging biblical chronology (p. 444-448). This is certainly an extreme stretch of the biblical language even in Camping's unique hermeneutic. To defend his use of multiple zero numbers as the ultimate criterion for correct chronology, Camping goes so far as to say that the errors in the Gregorian calendar were "incorporated . . . by the express intent of God" (p. 374). Apparently, Camping believes that God purposefully included an error in the Gregorian calendar so that Christ's birth could be in 7 B.C. instead of A.D. 1 in order to have exactly 2,000 years from 7 B.C. to A.D. 1994. Here again, Camping implies that God *fixes* history to bring forth the meaning of symbolic numbers. Camping conveniently attributes to God something that the Bible does not even address.

The Birth and Death Dates of Jesus

To support calculations similar to those above, Camping employs a very liberal use of the word *"about."* An example is noted in his interpretation of Luke 3:23 where the Greek literally reads: "Jesus was beginning to be about thirty years old." Despite this statement, Camping holds that Christ was born in late 7 B.C. and died in early A.D. 33. These dates require Camping to conclude that Christ was 38-39 when He died and 35-36 when He began His ministry. (It is commonly accepted that Jesus was in public ministry for 3 to 3 1/2 years.) The biblical evidence does not support such a conclusion. First, it is stretching the Greek language beyond reason to presume, as Camping does, that *"about thirty"* can refer to the age of 35-36, especially since Jesus' time on earth was confined to His thirties. If Jesus was 35-36 when He entered His ministry, then, abiding with the way the New Testament uses the word *"about,"* Luke would have said, *"Jesus was about thirty-five."* Other Scriptural references to the word *"about"* (Greek: "hosei" with numerals) do not stretch the perimeter of meaning far beyond the original point of reference (Luke 1:56; 9:28; 22:59; 23:44). Second, Luke's use of the Greek participle *archomenos* ("was beginning") shows that Jesus was just entering His thirties rather than being half-way through (age 35) or more than half-way (age 36) to completing His thirties. Third, there is no reason for Luke to be imprecise concerning his estimates since he himself claims that his testimony is very exact (Luke 1:3-4, 3:1-3). Fourth, we must also take into account that Luke had many reliable sources on which to depend, not the least of which is the inspiration of the Holy Spirit (Luke 1:1-2). Hence, an earlier date of Christ's death (such as A.D. 30, to which many scholars hold and which Camping acknowledges as a possibility) and a later date for His birth (4-6 B.C. or later) would make Jesus 29-31 when He started His ministry and fit much better with Luke's use of the clause *"was beginning to be about thirty."* These dates, of course, would send most of Camping's chronological calculations into a tail-spin, especially those of Daniel 9-12, which we will see later.

These remarks become extremely important since much of Camping's end-time calculations pivot off of 7 B.C. as the birth of Christ and A.D. 33 as the death of Christ. In order to arrive at 7 B.C. as the birth of Christ, Camping notes that Herod, who killed the babies two years and younger in Bethlehem, actually died in 4 B.C. According to the annals of Josephus, the first century A.D. Jewish historian, an eclipse of the moon occurred on the day of Herod's death, which according to astronomical records, occurred March 13, 4 B.C.[1] With this historical fact Camping concludes:

> Thus the birth of Jesus *could have been* at least two years earlier than 4 B.C. Also, a period of time *may have* elapsed between the killing of the babies by Herod and his death. Thus, we may be *reasonably certain* that on the basis of this evidence concerning Herod, Jesus must have been born between 9 B.C. and 6 B.C. [emphasis mine] (p. 372).

The use of 4 B.C. assumes that Josephus is accurate concerning the date of the lunar eclipse, or that the transmission of his works are unedited, or that there were no other eclipses in the proximity of Herod's death.

It is interesting to note here that Camping makes a *"reasonably certain"* conclusion from facts that *"could have been"* and *"may have"* been. Both the *"could have"* and the *"may have"* facts are desperately needed to decide with any degree of certitude that Jesus was born between 9 B.C. and 6 B.C., and certainly much more information is needed if one is going to conclude that he can pinpoint 7 B.C. as the precise date for Christ's birth. This conclusion becomes much more alarming when, in reading his books, 7 B.C. is touted by Camping as one of the most crucial dates for arriving at A.D. 1994 as the end of the world. It is extremely tenuous to base a precise date of the end of the world on *"could haves"* and *"may haves."*

Assuming Herod died shortly after he gave the decree for the slaughter of the children two years and younger, this could possibly place Jesus' birth in 6 B.C. However, this is assuming that Jesus was one of the children who was already two years old when Herod gave the command for the slaughter. The Bible does not specifically say that Jesus was two. He could have been anywhere from 1-24 months old. From the information he obtained from the Magi, Herod did not conclude that Jesus was two years old since he specifically ordered the killing of children "two years old *and under*" (Matt. 2:16). If he thought Jesus was exactly two, or very near two, it would not have been necessary to kill the babies who were three months old, six months old, one year old, etc. Herod, since he did not know exactly how old Jesus was, ordered the death of children two years and under to make certain that he did not miss killing the Christ child. Jesus did not necessarily have to be two years old when the slaughter took place. Most likely, he was much younger than two years. This means that Jesus could have been born in 4 or 5 B.C., or later if Josephus' dates are in error or wrongly recorded. In any case, there is much uncertainty concerning the year Jesus was born, especially since the Bible does not specify the year. There is certainly not enough biblical information to pivot off of 7 B.C. and project a date to the end of the world.

5

Choosing One's Own Beginning and Ending Dates for Biblical Time Spans

by Robert Sungenis

Not only does Camping tout zero-filled numbers as the ultimate criterion for correct biblical chronology, he also chooses the starting and ending points for his numbers. Essentially, Camping starts with what he believes is a significant biblical number and then simply finds two dates between which the number fits. These calculations seem very impressive because they fit so exactly. After the injection of the number between two dates, Camping stands back and marvels at how precisely the numbers of the Bible fit together and expects his audience to do the same. However, the wonder vanishes once we begin to unravel what is really happening in Camping's calculations. Because there are literally hundreds of biblical events from which to choose, such as birth and death dates, entrance and exit dates, blessing and judgment dates, feast dates, beginning and ending dates of reigns, dates of momentous or cataclysmic events, etc., it is very easy for one to find a significant event in the distant past and then project to an event in the future that is spanned by a large whole number with multiple zeros like 2,000, 4,000, or 7,000. All one has to do is start with several zeros, precede it by a numeral from 1 to 9, since the Bible uses all single digit numbers symbolically, and then find two dates between which the large number fits. Since there are so many biblical events from which to choose, and so many symbolic numbers at one's disposal, it is a relatively easy task to accomplish. At the same time, one can ignore all the time spans between two events that don't incorporate numbers with multiple zeros or that are not "symbolic." In this way everything appears so neat and orderly.

The Number 13

Related to the above scheme of numbers is Camping's predominant use of the number 13 which he believes represents "super fullness." Camping begins most of his end-time numerical theories by alerting us to the fact that there are exactly 13,000 years from the beginning of creation to the end of the world. The 13,000 years of the earth's existence supposedly demonstrates the fullness of God's work on earth. This symbolic meaning is precariously derived from the fact that the Bible uses the number 12 symbolically to demonstrate fullness. For example, the 12 tribes of Israel or the 12 Apostles refer to fullness. Camping takes this a step farther. Since there were actually 13 tribes (Joseph was divided into Ephraim and Manasseh) and 13 Apostles (Paul being the thirteenth), then the number 13 is similar to the number 12, only with richer meaning (p. 441). This kind of interpretation is completely contrived and unbiblical.

Regardless whether the number 13 symbolizes "super fullness," there is a glaring discrepancy in this calculation to which either Camping is oblivious or does not care to address. If 13,000 years is added to Camping's creation date of 11013 B.C. we do not come to the end of the world in A.D. 1994 but to A.D. 1988 (11,013 + 1988 - 1 = 13,000). A.D. 1988 is the beginning of Camping's Tribulation period, not the end of the world. Skirting this fact, in his books Camping consistently refers to 1988 as the "end of the world" (AYR: p. 29, 31, 221, 257, et al.). Only once in reference to the 13,000 years does Camping refer to 1988 as the beginning of a "judgment" period and not the end of the world (AYR: p. 316). It seems that Camping can make his calculations fit by juggling end points and definitions as well as numbers.

One of the more outlandish uses of the number 13,000 was in a recent radio broadcast over Camping's talk show, "Open Forum." Several days prior, Camping alerted his listening audience that he would soon be making a "special announcement." When the day came, Camping took a half-hour to explain that from the very day he received a loan to start Family Radio on February 4, 1959, through September 6, 1994, was exactly 13,000 days. September 6, 1994, is significant in Camping's scheme of things since he claims it is the last day of the "final Tribulation period" that started May 21, 1988. Camping claims that there will be an interlude of 9 to 21 days until Christ returns between September 15-27. Camping touted this information as further proof that God was totally behind the ministry of Family Radio like no other ministry on earth before or since. To Camping, the "super fullness" of God's gospel proclamation will have been embodied in Family Radio for 13,000 days, a number even God himself used for the duration of His full gospel proclamation to mankind at large for 13,000 years. From such bizarre claims, one cannot help but form the opinion that Camping thinks that God has exclusively chosen him to possess the gospel of salvation and that the fate of the world rests on his shoulders. May God have mercy on his soul.

Camping also likes *"extra special numbers"* like 153 from John 21 and 276 from Acts 27 because if one adds the successive integers $(1 + 2 + 3 \ldots)$ he will arrive at 153 and 276, respectively (p. 229, 504). Where the Bible substantiates using the addition of integers as proof of correct exegesis and chronology, Camping does not tell us. One wonders that if the addition of successive integers is such a valid biblical criterion for significant numbers, why are numbers like 28 (that is, $1 + 2 + \ldots + 7$), or 45 (that is, $1 + 2 + \ldots + 9$) which are also found in the Bible and follow the same pattern, categorized as "seemingly unimportant" by Camping (p. 228). This is a common occurrence in Camping's book — he alone decides which numbers are significant and how they will be used. If they fit into his numerical scheme, they become significant. If they do not, they are ignored.

One of Camping's supporters, Ernest Springer, while not fully endorsing Camping's dating, attempts to soften the inconsistencies of Camping's mathematical calculations. He writes, "Remember that it is a lot easier to twist words, even God's words, than it is to twist mathematics. The reason for this is that mathematics is governed by rules that do not allow for individual or personal preference. The same cannot be said of exegesis and hermeneutics."[1]

Contrary to what Springer says, as we have seen in the present chapter, numbers *can be manipulated* by individuals and for personal preference. The remainder of this critique will continue to show that it is just as easy to distort the Bible's numbers as it is to distort its prose and poetry.

6

Forcing Symbolic Meaning on Common Prime Numbers

by Robert Sungenis

In the book *Are You Ready?*, Camping includes a large section that shows 49 paths to the end of the world (p. 255-314). Usually, Camping starts with the birthdate of an Old Testament figure, calculates how many years transpire until Camping's presumed date of the end of the world, and then breaks the span of years down into single or double digit multiples, assigning a specific "spiritual" meaning to each number that coincides with his understanding of gospel truths. For example, according to Camping, Eber was born in 3617 B.C. The number of years from Eber's birth to A.D. 1994 is 5,610. Camping alerts us to the fact that the number 5,610 can be broken down into its prime number multiples of 2 x 3 x 5 x 11 x 17, representing: the Church (2), God's purpose (3), salvation (5), Christ's first coming (11), and heaven (17), respectively. From Camping's perspective this is quite impressive since he holds that such numbers are used consistently in the Bible to reveal gospel truths. But when examined very carefully, these calculations exhibit a gross manipulation of biblical numbers and the inclusion of non-biblical principles of interpretation. Camping has very scant and ambiguous biblical evidence to show that these numbers represent what he says they represent. It should also be kept in mind that previous allegorizing interpreters have assigned very different meanings to the same numbers. This is the natural course of events when 1) the Scripture does not delineate specific meanings for its numbers, and 2) men of different mindsets come to the Scripture with their particular symbolic biases and subsequently read them into the text.

As seen above, almost all of Camping's numerical theories are based on the idea that biblical time spans should be broken down into their "prime" number multiples. (A prime number is any number divisible only by itself and the number one). Hence, in the above calculation concerning Eber, the numbers 2, 3, 5, 11, 17 are the prime multiples of the number 5,610 since they cannot be divided any further. The glaring problem in this interpretive scheme, especially from one like Camping who claims that all interpretations must be validated from the Bible (p. 382), is that Camping, neither in *1994?* or *Are You Ready?* shows us: 1) where the Bible explicitly teaches that its numbers are to be broken down into prime numbers, and 2) where the Bible explicitly teaches that a series of numbers has a progressive symbolic meaning when used in combination with other "symbolic" numbers. Camping violates his own fundamental principle of interpretation by not citing chapter and verse that supports his prime number theory. Hence, according to his own exegetical requirements, the whole numerical scheme falls under its own weight.

A second glaring anomaly in Camping's time-span calculations is the obvious exclusion of large portions of the genealogical record. After Eber, Camping does not investigate the numbers of another person from the genealogical record of Genesis 11 until he gets to Terah. He conveniently leaves out Peleg, Reu, Serug, and Nahor. Apparently, Camping cannot make the time spans from their births till the end of the world fit any significant symbolic pattern, and thus they are ignored. This is a prime example of Camping's biased selectivity when he attempts to display the symbolic meaning of numbers. By what criterion are these names left out? Certainly Eber was no more historically significant than Peleg, Reu, Serug, or Nahor. In fact, it is Camping who claims that Peleg is a very significant person in the genealogical record since it was in Peleg's days that the earth was divided. (Camping holds that the continental shift started in Peleg's time as a judgment from God.) Certainly a judgmental event as momentous as the dividing of the continents would make Peleg's dating stand out and tie in somehow with the judgment at the end of the world. But there is no claim to such an idea in Camping's scheme since the numbers from Peleg's birth to the end of the world do not show any symbolic pattern. Indeed, using Camping's "actual" year calendar, the birth date for Peleg in 3153 B.C. to A.D. 1994 is a total of 5,146 years. The number 5,146, broken up into its prime numbers, is 2 x 31 x 83. Since Camping has not touted 31 and 83 as having any symbolic significance, Peleg is simply left out of the picture. Camping makes absolutely no mention of this absence in either of his books. If confronted with these kinds of anomalies, it is my guess that Camping will either say that God chose not to give Peleg's dating any symbolic significance, or that he (Camping) has not yet discovered the symbolic meaning of 31 or 83 (AYR: p. 181, 190). Very effectively, Camping will cover all his bases.

Another circuitous means that Camping uses to make his time spans fit is the employment of two ending dates for the end of the world, that is, A.D. 1994 and A.D. 1988, as well as the use of two different calendars, the "actual" years and the "calendar" years. Indeed, by the use of these four variables, Camping increases *fourfold* the possibility of making his time spans fit well enough to display his symbolic prime numbers. Throughout *1994?* and *Are You Ready?,* Camping shifts between using A.D. 1994 and A.D. 1988 as the ending point for his time spans that begin in the Old Testament. For example, on one page Camping claims that the birth of Seth, being in the year 10,883 B.C., is exactly 12,870 "years to the end of the world, *A.D. 1988*" (AYR: p. 258) [emphasis mine]. He then breaks 12,870 down into its prime number components: 3 x 3 x 10 x 11 x 13, giving a symbolic meaning to each number. The spiritual meaning is then made coherent in a well-fashioned sentence. Then on the next page, Camping uses Enoch's birthdate of 7106 B.C. and says that it is exactly 9,100 "years to the end of the world, *A.D. 1994*" [emphasis mine]. The 9,100 years is shown to be a multiple of 7 x 13 x 100, each with their own symbolic significance. The obvious question here is why Camping switches from using 1988 in Seth's calculation to 1994 in Enoch's calculation? Though Camping does not admit this to the reader, the reason he must make this switch is that he can't find any symbolic numbers within the time-span of Seth's birthdate in 10,883 B.C. and the end in 1994. The years between these two dates are 12,876 (10,883 + 1994 - 1 = 12,876). The number 12,876, broken down into it prime number multiples is: 2 x 2 x 3 x 29 x 37. Since Camping has never claimed a symbolic significance for the number 29 (AYR: p. 190), he cannot claim that this series of numbers is used symbolically. Hence, the ending date of 1994 is discarded in favor of 1988 which yields more familiar symbolic numbers, as seen above — only one of many times the switching from 1994 to 1988 and vice-versa takes place in Camping's calculations. By using these two dates, Camping vastly increases his chances of creating his symbolic prime numbers to impress his audience.

Regarding the number 37, Camping believes it has symbolic significance because Noah spent 370 days, rather than the expected 360 days, upon the ark. Since 370 is a product of 37 x 10, the number 37 becomes a number representing God's judgment. (Why the number 37 does not represent *salvation* since Noah is finally coming out of the ark, Camping does not explain. This shows the complete arbitrariness of his symbolic numbers — we get a hint of the reason below.) Camping concludes from this matchup that: "God deliberately kept Noah and his family in the ark an extra long time so that the number 37 would be prominently featured" (AYR: p. 205). Hence, not only does Camping believe that God fashions symbolic numbers from historical narratives, but he also *fashions historical events* based on symbolic numbers. Having assigned a symbolic meaning to the number 37, Camping then uses this meaning to interpret the number 666 in Revelation 13:18 (AYR: p. 206). Since 666 is a multiple of 3 x 6 x 37, Camping feels he has found the ultimate solution to this puzzling number. All this is possible, according to Camping, because God made Noah stay an extra 10 days on the ark.

As noted above, another switching that takes place in many of Camping's calculations is the replacement of "calendar years" with "actual years" and vice versa. The Bible gives no explicit validation for using two different calendars, yet Camping consistently uses these to prove his numerical formulas.

Seizing upon the fact that there is no year "0," Camping has created two different calendars for his numerical system. The actual years are the exact years between an Old Testament event and a New Testament event. Thus, from 10 B.C. to A.D. 10 is actually 19 years, not 20 years, since the year "0" does not exist. Conversely, there are, according to Camping's understanding, 20 "calendar" years between 10 B.C. and A.D. 10. The "actual" years will always be one less year than "calendar" years.

Using the same example from the birth of Seth and Enoch, Camping conveniently switches from using "actual" years in Seth's calculations to "calendar" years in Enoch's calculations. Why? Because if he used "calendar" years in Seth's calculations and "actual" years in Enoch's calculations no significant symbolic numbers would be exhibited. For example, the "calendar" years from Seth's birth date in 10883 B.C. to 1988 = 12,871. Breaking 12,871 down to its prime number multiples is 61 x 211. These are not symbolic numbers for Camping, thus they are ignored. Likewise, the "actual" number of years from Enoch's birth to 1994 is 9,099, as opposed to Camping's "calendar" years of 9,100. Breaking down 9,099 into its prime numbers is: 3 x 3 x 3 x 337. Since 337 is not symbolic for Camping, this series of numbers is ignored. This switching between "actual" years and "calendar" years appears many times in Camping's calculations.

To drive home this point even further, one can take almost any large digit number, add either 1994 or 1988 to it, use both "actual" years and "calendar" years, and one will be able to obtain Camping's symbolic numbers. Let's take an arbitrary number — one that is exactly between two of Camping's Old Testament dates. For example, Camping says that Serug's birthdate is 2675 B.C. and Nahor's birthdate is 2445 B.C. The date exactly between 2675 and 2445 is the year 2560 B.C. Now, let's run the number 2,560, which has no historical significance in Camping's dating, through the regiment of Camping's formulas to see if we can produce any "symbolic components."

	Actual Years	Calendar Years
1994 + 2,560 =	4,553 years	4,554 years
1988 + 2,560 =	4,547 years	4,548 years

If we break each resulting number into its prime multiples:

    4,553 = 29 X 157
    4,547 = 1 X 4,547
    4,554 = 2 x 3 x 3 x 11 x 23
    4,548 = 2 x 2 x 3 x 379

As noted by the resulting multiples of **2, 3, 11,** and **23,** we have easily arrived at Camping's symbolic prime numbers just by picking an arbitrary number and putting it through Camping's four scenarios. One of the scenarios, the "calendar" years to 1994, yielded these "symbolic" numbers. The point to be made in this exercise is that one can choose almost any multiple digit number and find Camping's "symbolic components" if one has enough formulas through which to run it. With almost every number I arbitrarily selected, I was able to produce Camping's symbolic numbers. Let's do it one more time.

Camping says Arphaxad was born in 4488 and Selah was born in 4050. The year halfway between these two dates is 4269. Setting up the grid we have:

	Actual Years	Calendar Years
1994 + 4,269 =	6,262 years	6,263 years
1988 + 4,269 =	6,256 years	6,257 years

If we break each resulting number into its prime multiples:

    6,262 = 2 x 31 x 101
    6,263 = 1 x 6,263
    6,256 = 2 x 2 x 2 x 2 x 17 x 23
    6,257 = 1 x 6,257

Again, by picking a completely arbitrary number, we are able to produce Camping's symbolic numbers, among them 17 and 23, which are two of the most highly significant to Camping.

After witnessing how easy it is to manipulate numbers, we begin to see that Camping's 49 paths to the end of the world are really not that impressive at all. Reaching a desired date by allowing himself four different formulas of calculation is hardly a stupendous achievement. In effect, the uncovering of such an open-ended scheme of dating can't help but make one skeptical of Camping's entire end-time theory.

7

The Improper Use of Old Testament Feast Days
by Robert Sungenis

Closely akin to his manipulation of numbers, Camping also makes convenient use of Old Testament feast days and laws, showing how they point symbolically to the end of time. It is true that various Old Testament feasts prefigured New Testament events, such as, the Old Testament Passover and Feast of Weeks prefigured the death of Christ and the descent of the Holy Spirit at Pentecost, respectively. It is also true that these two first century A.D. events occurred on the exact day they had been celebrated in ancient Israel. We recognize this one-to-one correspondence because the New Testament explicitly reveals it. From this limited correspondence, however, Camping hypothesizes that other Old Testament events, notably, the Jubilee festival, can be projected beyond the first century to the end of time. The Jubilee year was a time when all debts were canceled and slaves were returned to their families (Lev. 25). It is the only instance the Jubilee is mentioned in the Bible. Camping calculates that the Jubilee feast was celebrated every 50 years in Israel. According to Camping's chronology, 7 B.C., the year he claims Christ was born, was a Jubilee year. Camping then discovers that there are exactly 40 Jubilee periods (50 years for each period) from Christ's first coming in 7 B.C. to His second coming in A.D. 1994 (p. 517-521). Camping lauds the 40 Jubilee periods between 7 B.C. and A.D. 1994 as his most important discovery for dating the end of the world. Camping states: "Moreover, because the *single greatest focus* on 1994 as the year of Christ's return is the Jubilee information in the Bible, a further discussion of that event is included" (AYR: p. xxii) [emphasis mine]. Though at first sight this calculation seems impressive, as we have seen with other formulas used by Camping, he fails to disclose to his readers the most crucial piece of evidence to substantiate his claim: Where does the Scripture give specific validation for continuing the Jubilee clock past the Old Testament? Camping attempts to substantiate his claim as follows:

> Now we are in the New Testament. God assures us that the *spiritual application* of the Old Testament feast day goes on into the New Testament era. This is proven by the fact that fifty days after the Passover was the feast of weeks at which time the initial harvest was recognized as a special day called Pentecost. . . . Indeed, God is *clearly* demonstrating that Old Testament feast days have a *literal application* in the New Testament era. *But the application is not to be done by the church or by man's effort. It is to be done by God* (AYR: p. 22) [emphasis mine].

It is one thing to see the *"spiritual application"* of Old Testament feasts such as Passover and the Feast of Weeks fulfilled in New Testament events, but it is quite another thing to extend the literal calendar of Old Testament feasts into the New Testament, especially for the purposes of arriving at a supposed date for the end of the world some 2,000 years away. Granted, the Jubilee principle certainly has "spiritual application" in the New Testament, since the release of debt in the Jubilee year symbolized the release of man from sin and bondage. By the same token, the Feast of Tabernacles also has a spiritual application as it points to the gathering of the "harvest" of souls at the end of time (Matt. 13). Going beyond the available biblical information, Camping holds to a detailed chronology of the Jubilee feasts such that every 50-year period in the Gregorian or Julian calendar is a Jubilee fulfillment. Thus, 7 B.C., A.D. 44, A.D. 94, A.D. 144, A.D. 194, A.D. 1944, and A.D. 1994 were all Jubilee years that God used to track time in the New Testament until Christ returns. To extend a *detailed calendar* of the Jubilee period down 2,000 years of non-Jewish history until A.D. 1994 is a calculation the Bible simply does not even remotely address. Their literal reckoning being confined to the Old Testament, the Bible gives no credence to such New Testament chronological extension of its Jubilee feasts, nor is there any suggestion in the New Testament that time is charted by the use of such feasts. If anything, such feasts are categorically ignored (Col. 2:16; Gal. 4:10). For one who is quick to accuse others of fashioning doctrines without biblical foundation, Camping seems to have done the same with his detailed calendar extension of the Jubilee feasts. He has done exactly what he warned against in the above quotation, that is, allowing "man's effort," that is, Camping himself, to create a "literal application" of the Jubilee feast. God certainly makes no explicit indication in the Bible that He is continuing the literal Jubilee clock past the Old Testament.

In further analysis, we might ask why, even in Camping's scheme of things, he has settled on 40 Jubilees rather than 50? Fifty Jubilees would certainly tie in better with the fact that the Jubilee occurred every 50 years in the Old Testament. We must also remember that the 40 Jubilee periods are only significant in Camping's scheme of things if 7 B.C. was the birth of Christ. As noted previously, Camping has by no means given us certitude that 7 B.C. was the birth of Christ, especially since 7 B.C. cannot be proven from the Bible itself. Thus it seems rather presumptuous to say, as he is quoted earlier, that "the single greatest focus on 1994 is the Jubilee information in the Bible" if one cannot prove *from the Bible alone* that 7 B.C. was the birth of Christ.

It is also interesting to observe Camping's reasoning as to how he settles on A.D. 1994 rather than the forty-first Jubilee in A.D. 2044. Camping tells us that though A.D. 2044 is a candidate for the end of the world, it is discounted by the fact that the chronological pathways to A.D. 2044 are *less than half* of those that lead to 1994 (AYR: p. 315). This helps explain why

Camping's two books are so voluminous. In his mind, the more pathways he can create to a specific date the more certain we can be that that date is the end of the world. In effect, truth is claimed to have been discovered by taking a *head count* of the potential candidates. Is this the way the Bible teaches us to arrive at truth? Certainly not.

8

Claiming Special God-Given Knowledge for Oneself

by Robert Sungenis

One of Camping's strong and persistent beliefs which he feels gives him license to predict the return of Christ is that as the world approaches its end God will reveal precise knowledge of its timing to certain faithful individuals. Using Daniel 12:4 as a premise, Camping claims that the errors of previous end-time predictors are due to the absence of the "increased knowledge" of the Bible that he has apparently received from God (p. 328f). This reasoning also helps Camping to counter the clear language of Acts 1:7 that the "times and seasons" of the end are not for us to know. He claims that Acts 1:7 is not an absolute statement but a temporary veiling (p. 329). Camping develops this interpretation by claiming that the Greek construction of Acts 1:7 should be "of you" not "for you." The wording "of you," Camping claims, means that it was not God's purpose nor within the Apostles ability, at that time, to know the timing of the end, but that it would be possible for others to know it in the future. However, the Greek genitive *humon* coupled with the aorist infinitive *gnonai* is a "genitive of relationship" meaning that the timing of the end is not relatable to the Apostles. In other words, the timing of the end is something that does not belong in their possession at all. This analysis can be confirmed by consulting any Greek commentary that addresses the issue.

Camping also quotes from Daniel 12:10 and explains to us that the "enlightened" to whom this special knowledge is given refers to those who understand when the Tribulation will begin. Since only Camping and his followers believe the Tribulation started May 21, 1988, and that the end of the world will occur in September 1994, one wonders if implicitly Camping is telling the rest of Christendom that they are not true believers, either because God hasn't revealed this special knowledge to them or that they don't believe Mr. Camping when he tells them it is so. Realizing his predictions are controversial, Camping also quotes from Ezekiel 33:1-9 and explains that he is compelled to at least make the month and year of Christ's return known to save his own soul (p. 325).

Camping supports his contention that God is expecting him to look into the Bible to discover the timing of the end by an appeal to 2 Peter 3:12. In this passage Camping claims that the words *looking for* (KJV) specifies a "very intense looking" such that we are thereby instructed to "look" into the Bible intensely for information related to the date of the end. First, the passage does not say to "look" into the Scripture, rather, it says to look to the "coming of the day of God." In fact, we are also told to "look" (same Greek word) for "new heavens and new earth" in the next verse (2 Pet. 3:13). We look because we know *that* He will come, not *when* He will come. Second, the Greek word for "look" (*prosdokao*) is not a special word with an intense meaning. Although Camping appeals to its usage in Acts 28, the word is used 16 times in the New Testament by three different authors, denoting a normal looking forward or anticipation of an event. Camping is reading into the word the meaning he would like to see. Moreover, the word is never used in reference to peering into the numbers of the Bible nor the Bible itself. Other texts encourage us to read the Bible but not to find a date for the end.

Camping also appeals to 1 Thessalonians 5:2-4 to support his search for the timing of the end. Since verse 4 says the day of

His coming will not overtake believers as a thief, Camping claims that this Scripture is fulfilled as believers come to know the month and year of Christ's return. They will not be surprised because they know *when* He is coming. Besides the fact that the "day" is not the same as the month and year, a fair reading of the context does not in the least support such a view. The context has nothing at all to do with timing or chronology. It is contrasting the obedient from the disobedient. Those who are disobedient will by visited by Christ like a thief because they are not *spiritually* ready for Him, not because they do not know the exact timing of His return. Camping twists the passage in a desperate attempt to find biblical warrant for his end-time calculations.

Camping also cites the clause in Hebrews 10:25, "as you see the Day approaching." He claims that the only way this verse can make sense is if we know *when* the "day" will occur, the day referring to the second coming of Christ. He fails to show us how, then, it applies to the Hebrews to whom it was written. They certainly did not have to know the exact month and year of Christ's return in order to see the day approaching. In actuality, each day that went by brought them closer to the return of Christ and thus they could view His "approach" as being nearer than the previous day.

Contrary to Camping's claim, the prophecy of Daniel gives no suggestion that the understanding of his prophecy would be unfolded to certain individuals just prior to the second coming of Christ. If Camping were correct, then apparently God has chosen to hide this apocalyptic dating from the remainder of the Christian scholarly world today since no reputable theologian has ever documented that he agrees with Camping, or that God has given him the same month and year that Camping has found, or that God has given him the same interpretive method as Camping to begin calculating this specific dating. When compared to all the other established theologians of the world, past and present, the date of September 1994, and the method to arrive at that date, are unique to Camping. Camping seizes upon the absence of scholarly support as evidence that God does not give such knowledge to "apostate theologians" but has chosen to endow only Harold Camping with this special knowledge.

One person from Australia, Bruno Kolberg, claims in his

book, *The Final Tribulation . . . Days of Vengeance,* that the world will end in 1994.[1] Those who follow Camping claim that Kolberg had arrived at this date totally independent of Camping. I doubt this very much. Camping's teaching is available in Australia as it is all over the world. I also know the Camping and Kolberg parties have been in contact. This was confirmed at Camping's most recent debate in which some of his followers drove from California to Delaware, the location of the debate, with a truckload of Kolberg's books, sent by Kolberg from Australia for the purpose of giving free copies to interested parties. Similarly, many followers of Camping have calculated that the end will occur in 1994, some claiming to have done it independently of Camping. In reality, without being totally conscious of it, these people use a great deal of Camping's numerological framework and then enhance the dating with their own theories and formulas. It is quite easy. I used to dabble in it myself when I worked at Family Radio, and still retain my notes. The calculations, however, were never independent of Camping's thinking.

That Daniel is not suggesting that his prophecy will only be understood just prior to the second coming of Christ can be seen in the context. Already in Daniel 12:4, Daniel himself is told to "close up" (Hebrew: satham) and "seal up" (Hebrew: chatham). These Hebrew participles only state what is or shall be done, i.e., the prophecy shall remain until the time of the end. They denote the closing up and sealing which must be done by Daniel. Yet Daniel could not seal the prophecy till the end since he did not live to see the end. Hence, the closing up and sealing can only refer to the fact that the scroll must be preserved against any alteration or destruction of its contents so that it could be read at any time, right up until the end. This agrees with the practice of sealing documents in Hebrew culture. Both Hebrew words (satham and chatham) are used in this way in other passages (Isa. 8:16; Jer. 32:11,14). The reading of Daniel's prophecy would give strength and encouragement to God's people. This help is implied in Daniel 12:4, "Many will go here and there and be increased in knowledge" or Daniel 12:10, "The wise will understand." As indicated in Daniel 10:14, Daniel's prophecies concern what will happen to the people of Israel. Accordingly, Daniel 11 explains the details of the wars that will occur between Persia, Greece, Edom, Moab, Egypt, etc. The righteous people of Israel are comforted in that despite the upheaval caused by these warring nations, they will be preserved as recorded in Daniel 12:1-4. Reading and understanding Daniel's prophecies assure them of this divine protection. This comfort of God's people would continue right up until the "time of the end," that is, until Israel's final demise in the first century A.D.

Jesus himself indicated that Daniel's prophecy was already unfolding in Jesus' time as He made reference to the abomination of desolation recorded in Daniel 9-12. In Matthew 24:15, Jesus specifically said, *"Let the reader understand"* in reference to Daniel's prophecy. This parenthetical statement commanding the prophecy to be understood by the first century reader is an unequivocal clue to the timing of Matthew 24. The hearers and readers of the New Testament, beginning in the first century when oral and written revelation was circulating, were commanded to understand Daniel's prophecy by looking at the circumstances and events surrounding their generation, not to events in the distant future. In addition, the apostle John in the Book of Revelation specifically states: *"The revelation of Jesus Christ, which God gave him to show his servants what must soon take place . . . take to heart what is written in it, because the time is near* (Rev. 1:1-3), and *"Do not seal the words of the prophecy of this book, because the time is near"* (Rev. 22:10). Since Revelation is closely tied to the prophecies of Daniel, the command *"not to seal the words of the prophecy"* shows that their meaning was already being made evident in John's time. The fulfillment of these prophecies was not confined to the distant future, as Camping claims, but took place *soon* after John's writing of them and thus was known to the whole Church, not limited to one man in the twentieth century.

Unfortunately, if one challenges Camping that he can't do these kinds of things with the Scriptures, Camping, as he often did with me, will retort that his critics just don't understand the nature of the Bible. Because Camping has self-interpreted the Bible without any formal accountability his whole life, he has developed a thick theological insulation to protect himself from criticism. With his deep, authoritarian voice on the radio and a consistent flow of "us-them" polemical literature, Camping convinces many naive Christians that he is virtually the only one in our day blessed of God to understand the real meaning of the Bible.

One example of this tendency in *1994?* is seen in the following statement by Camping: "It should also be emphasized that this is not a time for theological debate. . . . The time for that argumentation is long past. There is no time to trust your pastor or your church. You must trust only in the Bible" (p. 534). One wonders why debating his claims is "long past" since *1994?* was published as recently as September 1992. Provocative books that predict the date of the end of the world deserve to be thoroughly debated, yet here Camping is shutting the door on such formal scrutiny before the book is even off the press. The book had not even been around long enough for a literary review, let alone an exhaustive investigation into his claims by competent and faithful scholars. In addition, it is quite audacious to make a blanket statement telling everyone to cease trusting in their pastor and church. The implication is very strong that only Camping's ministry is approved by God and everyone else is apostate.

In *1994?* Camping forms an impression of having superior interpretive abilities by first dazzling the reader with intricate numerical equations and then reinforcing his conclusions by stating that these equations are God-inspired. For example, at one point Camping is attempting to find the length of "the final Tribulation period" and states that the 3 1/2 days of Revelation 11:9, the 42 months of Revelation 11:2, the 70 years of Babylonian captivity, and the number 23 from the 2,300 days of Daniel 8:14 all have the common denominator of 42 since 3 1/2 days equals 84 hours, 70 years equals 840 months, and 23 years equals 8,400 days (84 divided by 2 equals 42). After this intricate display, Camping concludes: *"Isn't this a startling piece of information? God has interrelated the periods of three and a half days, forty-two months, twenty-three years, and seventy years by the common denominator forty-two"* (p. 237), [emphasis mine]. Here Camping invents a novel numerical relationship, one that is not specifically taught anywhere in the Bible, and then claims that *"God"* has given this to us. This is a perfect example of how Camping consistently fails to distinguish in the reader's mind what he has merely theorized and what God has actually done.

There is no evidence in the Bible that God bases the meaning or outcome of prophecy on common denominators.

Finally, as Camping claims to have been led to the knowledge of the timing of the end due to the fact that God is for the first time revealing this crucial information, it is a curious thing to listen to Camping's current "Family Bible Study" on Family Radio and witness him change his mind on certain details of his interpretation. For example, in a recent "Family Bible Study" Camping changed his mind and said that there may not be a literal darkening of the sun and moon nor a worldwide earthquake on September 7. Prior to this he was adamant that a literal darkening and earthquake must occur. Now Camping suggests that the darkening may only be spiritual, that is, a time when the light of the gospel is taken away and no one else can be saved. In place of this, Camping postulates that there may be a disruption of the earth's magnetic field which would cause total chaos and give a sign to the world that the end is near. Many other such details of his interpretation have similarly been changed. We wonder that if it is God who is suddenly revealing the details of the end to Camping, why is it that God is changing His mind on some of these details? Is this the way prophets have always received revelation from God or is this just another indication that Camping's theories are merely the product of his fallible interpretation of the Bible that needs to be saved from contradiction from time to time? In another light, if Christ does not come back in September 1994 then it can be safely said, and Camping should be the first to admit this, that God was *never* leading him to know the timing of the end in the first place. The haunting question that he will have to answer is: If it was not God who was leading him, then who was it?

9

Employing a Faulty View of the Church

by *Robert Sungenis*

In all of Camping's interpretation of prophecy there is one grand theme that keeps repeating itself over and over again. Camping firmly believes that the New Testament *"external"* Church will become apostate. When a particular individual or denomination seems to reject what he feels is correct doctrine, Camping will explain these localized departures from the faith as a sign of the inevitable apostasy of the external Church. According to Camping, May 21, 1988, was the beginning of the worst apostasy the Church has ever encountered, which will end some 2,300 days later with judgment day in September 1994. The *"eternal"* Church, on the other hand, is composed of the true believers from all the denominations that cannot lose their salvation and thus will remain faithful to the end. Camping considers himself, and his followers, in the eternal Church, and puts virtually everyone else who disagrees with him in the external Church.

In a Family Radio 1986 pocket prayer calendar, it states the following: "Family Radio is a family of believers (God's family) serving together, praying together and supporting together, the sending forth of the Gospel into all the world by way of radio. . . . ARE YOU A MEMBER OF GOD'S FAMILY?" This statement certainly makes a very strong implication that Family Radio is virtually the only place on earth where God's family now resides.

Camping claims that "in the Tribulation period Christ will become the enemy of the Church and will use Satan to 'kill' the true believers" (p. 198). This "killing" occurs when Christians are forced to depart from their churches due to false doctrine. This has become a self-fulfilling prophecy for Camping since he recently left the Christian Reformed Church in Alameda, California, which he had been attending for over two decades. It may be no coincidence that Camping left this church in the year 1988 — the year that supposedly began the "Tribulation period."

As a member and major contributor of that church, Camping had developed a high degree of influence, not to mention that he was well-known due to the media spotlight he enjoyed with Family Radio. Many years ago the church split over the doctrine of Charismatic gifts, Camping being highly instrumental in the controversy. In the early 1980s the church called a new pastor, Rev. Jack Huttinga. Upon his arrival, Camping and Huttinga were soon at odds with one another over various doctrinal issues. Finally, the elders of the church asked Camping to take a temporary leave from teaching the adult Sunday school. Camping refused and subsequently left the church with about 100 followers, mostly from the Sunday school class.

In a recent conversation with Scott Temple, Camping claimed that the whole controversy was started because the new pastor was "jealous" over Camping's large following in the church. However, as a personal witness to the exchange between Camping and Huttinga, I can attest that it was Camping who consistently goaded the latter with his polemical rhetoric. Camping did not try to work with the new pastor but was an antagonist from the beginning.

In his present studies Camping's bad experience with his former church colors many of the illustrations he uses to explain the apostasy of the Christian church at large today. Later in the conversation with Scott Temple, Camping said it was "very interesting" that the decision by his church elders to ask him to take a temporary leave from teaching the Sunday school class came "exactly two weeks after May 21, 1988" — the beginning of his so-called "Tribulation period" when Christians would be "forced from their churches."

Camping often remarks that he frequently gets letters from his listeners saying that they have "searched and searched and they cannot find a true church anywhere." Camping uses this evidence as proof that the Church at large is apostate. But what else is to be expected when Camping teaches them his narrow and esoteric gospel, and brands every other church that does not follow his teachings as a false gospel?

Many of his radio listeners have also left their churches since Camping has strongly suggested that they do so.

The most glaring anomaly concerning Camping's Tribulation period that supposedly started May 21, 1988, is that he offers virtually no solid evidence showing a difference between events prior to May 21, 1988, and events immediately after that date. In his books, Camping attempts to highlight the evils of the world to support his views, but it is obvious when one looks at the world objectively that the same evils exist after 1988 as existed prior. If the Tribulation period, described in Matthew 24:21 as, *"great distress unequaled from the beginning of the world until now"* is occurring at the present moment, there is certainly no visible evidence that substantiates such a phenomenon, at least not from events occurring in 1987. Matthew 24 specifies the traumatic, instantaneous, and distinct difference between the days prior to the Tribulation and the actual Tribulation, something Camping's theory does not provide. Along these lines, Camping also believes that May 21, 1988, was the fulfillment of the prophecy in Revelation 20:7-8 concerning the loosening of Satan to go out and deceive the nations. In turn, Camping believes that the battle of Armageddon and the battle of Gog and Magog (Ezek. 38-39; Rev. 16:20) is now taking place. If these things are so, again we would ask what evidence is there for proof? Certainly the fall of atheistic communism and the flood of the gospel into Russia and the East doesn't support such a theory. Camping attempts to answer this anomaly by claiming that: 1) the time and effects of the loosening of Satan and the Tribulation period are very similar to the time and effects when one is saved. Camping postulates that since we do not know when the Spirit actually enters our life, nor can we see all the effects of His working in us, similarly we would not have immediately seen the working of Satan nor the trauma of the Tribulation period on May 21, 1988 ("Family Bible Study," July 1, 1994). In brief, Camping has used an unbiblical and illegitimate comparison. The Bible never compares the timing and effects of the Spirit's work in salvation with the loosening of Satan and the Tribulation period. These are two entirely different events. By slipping this falla-cious yet convincing comparison into the argument, Camping makes the casual listener accept the matchup and conclude that the Tribulation period may not be immediately noticeable at all. This is *not* the impression given in Matthew 24:15-25. 2) Camp-ing claims that the Tribulation period is spiritual — a time when *"very few"* people are receiving salvation because the *"true gos-pel"* (as defined by Camping) has been silenced by Satan (p. 236). Some have countered with the fact that there seem to be just as many people believing and being baptized as there were in 1987. Camping would retort (as he has done many times on his radio programs) that it only appears that way. When they appear to be receiving Christ, they are actually receiving Satan because he is the master deceiver. According to Camping, the gospel that most Russians are receiving is a false gospel. Of course, Camping does not say this is true if it is *his* version of the gospel that they are being asked to receive.

It is interesting to note the evolution in Camping's thought on this issue. For many years Camping taught that the Tribula-tion period would not be noticeable by most people since it was, in essence, a "spiritual" tribulation. In past years Camping taught that the Tribulation was a time when no one could be saved. Though many would be claiming to receive Christ, Camping in-sisted that no one could be saved because the time of salvation would have ended. A few years ago he shifted his position and started to teach that people could still be saved during the Tribu-lation period. This may have been due to the fact that Camping's own family and friends were continuing to have children past May 21, 1988. Regardless of his exact reasoning, the problem with this new formulation is that his Tribulation period is not precisely defined. Since the salient features of Christendom and the world are much the same after 1988 as prior, that leaves Camping with the task of defining the Tribulation period based preponderantly on the results of his numerical calculations. Hence, there may be no practical differences between 1987 and 1988, but to Camping there is a chronological difference. May 21, 1988, must be the start of the Tribulation because, he insists, the numbers of the Bible demand it. Again, history is altered so symbolic numbers can take precedence.

Since Camping believes that Satan has been loosed from the bottomless pit (Rev. 20:1-3) to appear in the Tribulation period of May 21, 1988, to September 6, 1994, this also means that the predictions of the coming of the "Antichrist" must also be fulfilled simultaneously (1 John 4:3; 2 Thess. 2:3). Since there is no person yet alive who fills all the requirements of the Antichrist, Camping claims that the Antichrist is not a person but is Satan himself. Camping tries to prove this by an appeal to the language of 1 John 4:3. He purports that because the verse says the Antichrist is, a) "coming" and b) is "already in the world," then the Antichrist cannot refer to a person since no human being could be alive in John's time and still be alive today. Here is another instance in which Camping's ignorance of the Greek language can produce such erroneous interpretations. In 1 John 4:3 the Greek literally reads: "And every spirit which does not confess the Jesus is not of God, and this is *the* of the antichrist" [emphasis mine]. Though this is a bit awkward in English, it is an exact rendition of Greek. Notice that the Greek adds the article *"the"* before *"of the antichrist."* We do not speak or write this way in English. In Greek, this article demands a referent or compliment. The referent is the word *"spirit"* in the same sentence. This is why most translations, even the King James Bible that Camping uses, render the clause as: *"and this is the spirit of antichrist."* Since John is dealing with "spirits" who are recognized as to what they are by their confession, this translation makes perfect sense. The "spirits of antichrist" are the false prophets of John's day. Further, in John's other uses of the word "antichrist," the same sense of "the spirit of antichrist" is implied (1 John 2:18,22; 2 John 7). Thus, 1 John 4:3 does not mean that the Antichrist, whoever he is, must be able to live in John's time and also live in our time. Without a specific Antichrist, however, Camping's Tribulation period is quite impotent.

In Camping's view, one of the chief signs of the apostasy of the New Testament external Church is the existence of the phenomenon of tongues (p. 178-189). Tongues are supposedly the last "testing program" from God for the Church to see if they will remain faithful to the Bible alone, and according to Camping, the Church is miserably failing this final test. In arriving at this conclusion, Camping often remarks that long ago he struggled with how one could distinguish between false teaching and true teaching. He came to the firm conclusion that any revelation obtained outside the Bible was a product of a false gospel. Naturally, since tongues speakers claim to be receiving revelation from God outside the Bible, Camping categorically brands them as a false gospel. Since many denominations see tongues as a valid gift for today, Camping's reproach is directed to a wide audience.

Camping once told a friend of mine and myself, when I first arrived at Family Radio in 1982, that he expected God to make Pat Robertson president of the United States in 1984. Since Pat Robertson believes in tongues and miracles and is politically active, as president, Camping thought that this would be the best way that Satan could make tongues proliferate worldwide.

Whether tongues is a valid gift for today is not at issue in this study. What is at issue is the hermeneutic of Harold Camping. Camping forms his opinion of tongues, and other forms of extra-biblical revelation, by concentrating on one particular passage of Scripture. For many years Camping has used Revelation 22:18 (*"I warn everyone who hears the words of the prophecy of this book: If anyone adds to them, God will add to him the plagues described in this book."*) to teach that once the last book of the Bible was completed then God would not give any more revelations (AYR: p. 46-49). Though Camping touts his discovery of Revelation 22:18 as the ultimate solution to determine truth from error, the problem with using this verse to prove his case is that it simply begs the question. ("Begging the question" is a fallacy in logic in which one uses as proof a proposition that he has not first proven to be true.) *Nowhere does the New Testament indicate that Revelation is the last book of the Bible.* Since his own standards require Camping to validate every doctrine about the

Bible from the Bible, then because the Bible does not state which books were first or last, consequently, using Revelation 22:18 to prove his case is totally misleading and inappropriate. (See Appendix I for further information on Revelation 22:18-19.)

The most unfortunate thing in this whole matter is that, based on his view of Revelation 22:18, Camping has told innumerable people that they are going to hell.

In order to support his view that the New Testament church will become apostate, Camping makes a direct parallel between the demise of national Israel in the Old Testament and the falling away of the Church at the end of the New Testament period. Because there are various parallels between the Old and New Testaments, Camping presumes that the New Testament church will necessarily follow the precise degree of apostasy as the Old Testament nation of Israel. As would be expected, most of Camping's "proof texts" for the supposed apostasy of the New Testament church are taken from the Old Testament references to Israel. First, it directly contradicts Jesus' statement in Matthew 16:18 that *He* would build His church and *the gates of hell would not prevail against it*. Camping tries his best to downplay Jesus' statement and sidetrack the reader from its full import (p. 120, 156). One of Camping's explanations is that the Church Jesus protects is only the "spiritual Church of the elect." This interpretation falls in line with his spiritualization of most biblical passages. Camping fails to see that the Church is just as much physical and visible as it is spiritual and invisible. The word "church" is used over 100 times in the New Testament, not once referring to a purely spiritual Church. Christ loves and protects His physical Church even as a husband loves and protects his physical wife (Eph. 5:22-33). Camping has a strong tendency to fall into the Gnostic heresy of disdaining the physical Church and the physical world. This is one reason why he constantly spiritualizes the biblical text.

Camping's attempts to make an exact comparison between ancient Israel and the New Testament church are futile based on one simple fact: Israel was never given the eternal promise of protection that was given to the New Testament church. Though there are similarities between Israel and the New Testament church, there is not the one-to-one correspondence that Camping forces upon the relationship. It is precisely because Israel failed in the old covenant that Christ came with the new and better covenant that He would secure forever. Jesus told the Apostles, "I am with you always, even to the very end of the age" (Matt. 28:20). This means He would never leave them without the protection He promised for the Church in Matthew 16:18. Second, examples of churches with spiritual problems that are given in the New Testament are localized cases, such as the various churches mentioned in Revelation 1-3 or the Corinthian or Galatian church mentioned in Paul's epistles. However, there are no passages that speak of the apostasy of the *whole* New Testament church as Camping would have us believe. Though there will be intermittent and isolated departures from the true faith, the Church at large will remain triumphant simply because Jesus promised it would be so.

Camping often points to Revelation 13:7-8 to prove that the apostasy involves the whole Church throughout the entire world. But this passage is not speaking of the apostasy of the Church, but of the whole world of non-Christians who never were in the Church yet consistently attack the Church. The fact that they *"worship the beast"* means the same thing, for example, as worshipping the *"god of this world"* (2 Cor. 4:4; Rom. 16:20). There is a clear distinction in Revelation 13:6-8 between Christians and non-Christians; not between a faithful portion of the Church and an apostate portion of the Church. The New Testament never categorizes the Church as apostate, rather, it points out 1) those within the Church who fall away, and 2) those who are non-Christians and thus not part of the Church.

Because of his unique interpretations of the Bible and his negative experience with churches in general, Camping has developed an utter contempt for the modern day church. Rather than separating the good from the bad, Camping has washed his hands of the whole affair and declared the entire world evil and the entire Church apostate. As a result, Camping's interpretations of the Bible become overwhelmingly *judgment-centered* rather than *Christ-centered.* This is especially evidenced as Camping sees prophecies of the "Tribulation period" all over the Old Testament. Upon close examination, these texts are not in the least concerned with such an event.

10

Changing from One Form of Interpretation to Another

by Robert Sungenis

One of the key dimensions of Camping's interpretations in regards to prophecy is the prerogative he gives himself to arbitrarily switch from literal to spiritual interpretations, and vice versa, whenever it suits his apocalyptic agenda. If he can't make it fit literally, he will spiritualize it; if he can't make it fit spiritually, he will literalize it. Here are some examples of this type of exchange evident in *1994?*

The 11 Days Journey

In remarking on the 11-day journey of the Israelites in Deuteronomy 1:2, Camping concludes that it is impossible for this to refer to a literal 11-day journey. Hence, this verse becomes a candidate for Camping's spiritualization, and as if by magic, it is turned into 11,000 years. Camping then uses this 11,000-year period as convincing proof of his creation date of 11013 B.C. and his assumed date for the birth of Christ in 7 B.C. since they are exactly 11,000 years apart (p. 360-369). As noted previously, in Camping's mind, time spans that incorporate large whole numbers with two or three zeros tacked on have great symbolic significance and virtually prove that he is on the right track with his predictions. Nowhere does the Bible teach such numerical formulas to calibrate correct chronology.

Daniel's 21 Days

Camping does a similar exegesis of the 21 days of Daniel 10:2. To set up the leap into the spiritual meaning of the number 21, Camping tells us that 21 is a combination of 7, which symbolizes *perfection*, and 3, which is the number of God's *purpose*. He also tells us that the number 1,000 is significant because it represents the *completeness* of God's program. Hence, 3 x 7 x 1,000, which equals 2,100, becomes a very significant number. The final jump from Daniel's 21 days to Camping's 2,100 years is accomplished by three other facts to which Camping alerts us. The first is that a literal 21 days cannot fit into the historical context of Daniel 10. Second, Michael the archangel is really Christ. Last but not least, since Psalm 90:4 says that a thousand years in God's sight is as yesterday, then a day can be interpreted as a thousand years. Putting all these facts together, Camping proposes that Daniel was using 21 days to give parabolic information concerning 2,100 years. The 2,100 years is then used to bridge the time span between Abraham's circumcision, which Camping had already figured out earlier as 2068 B.C., to the crucifixion of Christ in A.D. 33 (who is supposedly Michael the archangel). In addition, Camping also uses 2067 B.C., the birth of Isaac, adds 2,100 years and arrives at A.D. 34, another significant date in his scheme since, as noted previously, there is a difference of one year between actual years and calendar years (p. 348).

After witnessing this convoluted exegesis, one wonders what limits there are to this unique form of interpretation. Here is another instance of making the Scripture conform to a preconceived notion of biblical chronology. The thinking process that occurred in Camping's mind to initiate this whole calculation probably went something like this: He had two dates, 2068 B.C. and A.D. 33, which he felt were very significant. He happened to notice that there were exactly 2,100 years between these two points. Since this "symbolic" number incorporated at least two zeros it was highly significant. He then searched the Bible for the number 2,100 but the closest he came was the 21 days of

Daniel 10. Then it was only a matter of spiritualizing 21 days into 2,100 years and Camping is able to show his audience how precisely the numbers of the Bible fit together.

Flaws in his logic almost jump out at the discerning reader. First, Camping does not tell us why the 21 days of Daniel 10:2 do not fit into the historical context, except to say that Daniel 10:1 suggests it was a *"long time."* Since 21 days is not a relatively long time, Camping feels justified in transposing it into 2,100 years. But the Hebrew original of Daniel 10:1, which Camping does not recognize, literally says, *"great conflict,"* not *"long time"* and thus the verse has nothing to do with chronology.

Second, Camping's leap from 21 days to 2,100 years is precariously supported by a reference to *"a thousand years as yesterday"* in Psalm 90:4. This verse, however, is not giving us a treatise on how to understand the numbers of the Bible but on God's conception of time relative to us. When it is to his advantage, Camping does not hesitate to interpret pure metaphors very literally.

Third, to say that 3, 7, and 1,000 are significant symbolic numbers is easy. One can always find significant features to any biblical number since the Bible uses every numeral from 1 to 9 in symbolic contexts. No one would deny that they have some symbolic significance, but we would most assuredly argue against how Camping distorts their significance to fit into his numerical scheme.

Fourth, on what basis is Michael the archangel equated to Christ? Just because Michael's name means, "who is like God" or because he is called, "the great prince" (Dan. 12:1) does not give us an adequate basis for a transposition. There are many Hebrew names that incorporate an identity with God and other personages that are called "prince" (Dan. 10:20-21) but this does not mean that they are God. "Prince" is from the Hebrew "sar" meaning: head, official, ruler, leader, etc. It refers to the fact that Michael is a great leader among other leaders. In addition, Daniel 10:13 says Michael is *one* of the chief princes, not the only one. In addition, there are many Scriptures that negate identifying Michael with Christ which are not addressed by Camping (Jude 9; Rev. 12:5-7).

Camping also believes that the angel Gabriel is God: "One

week before he made the startling announcement now published in *1994*? Harold Camping said, 'The Scripture teaches that Michael the archangel is God, and I believe the Scripture is also clear that Gabriel is God.' " This is a perfect example of what happens when one gives himself license to spiritualize the biblical text at will. Black is no longer black — it has become white.

Fifth, as noted previously, one of the major problems in Camping's use of numbers is the arbitrary starting and ending points he picks to make his "significant" numbers fit. For the 2,100 years seen above, Camping conveniently picks the date of Abraham's circumcision and Christ's crucifixion and then marvels at how precisely 2,100 years fits in between these two dates. This accomplishment is easy when one chooses the beginning and ending dates as well as the means to find the spiritual significance of the numbers they encompass. With this amount of license one can make the numbers of the Bible say virtually anything he wants. Besides, where in Daniel's entire prophetic revelation does he ever mention or imply a reference to Abraham?

Ezekiel's 390 Years

Camping uses the same type of interpretation in Ezekiel 4:5-6. Because he can't figure out how the 390 years for Israel's judgment and the 40 years of Judah's judgment fit into the chronology of Ezekiel's time period, Camping concludes that the only way to understand these numbers is by spiritualizing them. Camping then jumps to the conclusion that the 390 years are actually 3,900 years of judgment since multiples of 10 have the same spiritual significance as their divisor. Then, Camping must find a beginning and ending point for this 3,900 year period. Camping begins by hypothesizing that God's judgment will be upon Israel till the end of time, which in turn makes 1994 the ending date for the 3,900 years. The beginning date would then take him back to 1907 B.C. (A.D. 1994 - 3,900 = 1907 B.C. in "actual" years). To substantiate the significance of 1907 B.C. as the beginning of the 3,900 years, we are told that this is the year when Jacob wrestled with God, and hence, was the actual "beginning" of the nation of Israel and, in turn, the beginning of God's judgment upon Israel. With a few verses describing the nation's sins, Camping tries to convince us that God's judgment has been on Israel from the time that God wrestled with Jacob and extends for 3,900 years to 1994. With the 40 years of Ezekiel 4:6, Camping proposes that this can actually be 4,000 years, of which the starting point would be 2007 B.C. and transpire till its ending point in A.D. 1994. The year 2007 B.C. is said to be a valid starting point because it was the year of Jacob's birth and thus another "beginning" for Israel (p. 448f).

Here is another instance in which Camping defaults to the spiritualized interpretation to make the numbers fit into his theory. Not finding an historical solution to the numbers, Camping sees nothing wrong with adding a few zeros to a number to bring him to the date of 1994. But more importantly, Camping is not consistent to his own dates. He previously told us that the beginning of Israel began at the circumcision of Abraham in 2068 B.C. (p. 350). Then he told us that the beginning of Israel started with the birth of Jacob in 2007 B.C. (p. 444, 456). Then he told us that the beginning of Israel started in 1907 B.C. when Jacob wrestled with God (p. 452). It becomes obvious that these dates are not chosen because they give us the precise beginning of Israel but because they will allow his spiritualized use of biblical numbers to always end up at 1994 A.D. As noted previously, with so many events and symbolic numbers from which to choose, it is easy for Camping to juggle these dates to arrive at a predetermined end.

In further inquiry, we might ask why Ezekiel's judgment is made to refer to a time thousands of years in the past when it is clear from the context that God is dealing with the time period of Ezekiel. Just because Camping can't find an historical solution to the 390/40 year period does not mean that it does not exist. We would also question why Camping does not take into account the fact that Ezekiel specifies both a judgment on Israel and a judgment on Judah, which at the time of Ezekiel were two separate nations. Camping conveniently lumps both of these nations together under the heading of Israel, and then allows himself to begin the "judgment" in Jacob's lifetime when they were one people (p. 452).

11

Dazzling the Reader with Numerous Chronological Formulas

by Robert Sungenis

The Number 23

Camping does a similar lumping together in his listing of the kings of Israel and Judah, remarking that from the time of King Saul the nations of Israel and Judah had rejected God and were always under His judgment. Because the number 23 is touted by Camping to be the "number of judgment," the 23 kings from Saul to Zedekiah (Judah's kings) or from Saul to Hoshea (Israel's kings) are said to typify the final Tribulation period, which started May 21, 1988, the supposed beginning of God's judgment on the New Testament external Church for its apostasy (p. 225). Besides the overt spiritualizing that is going on here, what Camping doesn't explain in this apparently neat gathering of numbers is how the reigns of David and Solomon, not to mention the other good kings of Judah, can be considered as being under God's judgment when these reigns, according to the commentaries in the Book of Chronicles, were some of the most God-glorifying times in the nation's history? Rather than let the Chronicles give the divine perspective of the kings of Israel and Judah, Camping allows his understanding of the number 23 to dictate the interpretation and release his penchant for judgmental analysis.

If one is not careful to balance Scriptures which portray a negative slant on a particular individual or group with those that give a more positive slant, he would probably see, as Camping does, all of Israel's history as bleak, sinful, and being under God's judgment. But one must learn to synthesize these accounts as Chronicles does with Kings. Chronicles gives a much more positive account than Kings. In other instances, if one were to read the account of Samson in Judges 13-16, which makes Samson appear like a spiritual spoiled brat, without reading the positive slant recorded in Hebrews 11:32-40, he could get the wrong impression of the man. The same might be said of Jephthah who killed his daughter, or Jacob who was consistently deceitful, or even David who committed adultery and murder, according to the Old Testament accounts.

In the addendum to his book, Camping reassures us of the significance of the number 23 by pointing out that 1994 is one of only seven dates between 1949 and 2399 that if added up by place holdings (that is, 1 + 9 + 9 + 4), will equal 23. The liberal use of the number 23 is a perfect example of the artificial elevation of the significance of numbers in all of Camping's interpretations. Numbers take on a life of their own. At the expense of ignoring the plain meaning, numbers are frequently used as the main criteria to determine the final exegesis of a biblical text.

Because of their precise nature, there are dazzling arrangements one can create with numbers. To see how easily this can be done, I recommend the book by Gyles Brandreth entitled *Number Play*.[1] One of the main reasons that after a little investigation Camping's numbers lose their dazzle is that he is merely assigning arbitrary spiritual significance to common mathematical puzzles and calculations.

The number 23 is also featured in Camping's estimation of the number 1,955. Since there are exactly 1,955 years between A.D. 33 (the death of Christ) and A.D. 1988 (the beginning of Camping's Tribulation period), 1955 becomes a very significant number to Camping. Here again, Camping chooses the beginning and ending points of his calculation and then bridges them by a supposedly significant symbolic number. Unlike most of Camping's "bridgings" which incorporate whole numbers with several zeros, other numbers without zeros are used after they are broken down into their prime number multiples. For example, we are alerted to the fact that 1,955 is a combination of 5 x 17 x 23. Each of these numbers are extolled to be significant since Camping believes that "5" is the number of grace or judgment, "17" is the number of heaven, and "23" is the number of judgment. As with most of his symbolic numbers one will notice that Camping merely vacillates between the concepts of *judgment* or *salvation* when assigning meaning to numbers. This is a very easy thing to do and yet appears so profound to the average reader. These particular numbers are important because the aspects associated with them, namely, grace, judgment, and heaven, are said to be taking place between A.D. 33 and A.D. 1988 as the gospel is preached to the world. Camping whizzes these numbers by the reader and relies on the sheer profundity of the multiplication to validate his use of them. But nowhere does the Bible display or validate such multiplication of "symbolic" numbers to verify truth, nor is the number 1,955 featured anywhere in the Bible.

To show the complete arbitrariness of Camping's use of numbers, during his "Family Bible Study" (December 17, 1993), Camping claimed that the number 23 can sometimes be used in blessing contexts. This was said in reference to the incorporation of the number 23 in the joyous occasion of the completion of Solomon's temple (2 Chron. 7:10). True to form, however, Camping turned this into a judgment context before the program was over.

As noted earlier, the number 23 is most significant in Camping's estimation of the length of the so-called Tribulation period. Claiming that Daniel 8 is not concerned with the historical proximity of Daniel's time, Camping views the whole chapter as a prophecy of the end of the world. Hence, the 2,300 days of Daniel 8:14 become the time period between May 1988 and September 1994. Assuming for the sake of argument that Daniel 8 is even speaking of the end of the world, there are two anomalies that would cast much doubt on Camping's utter dependence on the 2,300 days. First, the inspired original Hebrew of Daniel

8:14 did not contain vowel pointings on the consonants, thus the number may not have been 2,300 at all. The vowel pointings were added by the Masorites in the first millennium B.C. in order to help in what they thought was the proper pronunciation of the Hebrew word. If a slight variation of vowel pointing is used for the Hebrew word "elep," the number could just as well be 1,300 instead of 2,300. It is very plausible that the 1,300 day period is the proper form since it would be much closer to the 1,290 days or 1,335 days of Daniel 12:11-12. This would answer the conflicts in the timing of the taking away of the daily and the subsequent desolation that are evident when one attempts to coincide 2,300 days with these events. In any case, Camping cannot be certain that the writer of Daniel was intending to mean 2,300, yet his whole theory concerning the length of his Tribulation period is based on this number. This is compounded by the fact that the number 2,300 is not mentioned in the rest of the Bible in connection with a Tribulation period nor any other event. For a treatment on this possibility, see *Biblical Hermeneutics* by Milton S. Terry.[2]

The difference in the two is between the Hebrew "dual" and "masculine plural" of the word "elep," of which the latter is a general form for "thousand" or "thousands," whereas the former is the only Hebrew way to say "two thousand." Terry also gives an extensive treatment on the improper use of "symbolic" numbers.

It should be noted that no other theologian throughout Christian history has understood the 1,300 or 2,300 days of Daniel 8:14 as referring to a Tribulation period at the end of time. Most have understood it to refer to the exploits of Antiochus Epiphanes who desecrated the Jewish sanctuary. Some have said that the 2,300 "evenings and mornings" refer to the temple sacrifices that were offered twice per day, once in the evening and once in the morning. Thus, there would have been 1,150 whole days with 2,300 sacrifices (1,150 x 2 = 2,300). The 1,150 days would coincide more closely with the other time periods mentioned in Daniel's prophecy.

The second anomaly caused by the use of the 2,300 days is that it doesn't quite fit into Camping's own numerical scheme. As airtight as he tries to make this number appear, Camping ends up having to reinterpret a few verses to make the 2,300 days co-incide with previous calculations. Camping claims that the 2,300 days starts on May 21, 1988. The ending point comes to September 6, 1994. This date is between 9 and 21 days shy of his pre-dicted end of the world on September 15-27. Though he does not admit this fact to followers of years past, the 9-21 day gap is a problem for Camping since he has stated repeatedly in the past that the Tribulation was to be the *last* event prior to the second coming of Christ. Camping attempts to answer this anomaly by claiming that the phrasing of Mark 13:24-27 ("But in those days, after the tribulation, the sun shall be darkened. . . . And they shall see the Son of Man coming in the clouds . . .") includes an inter-val of time (9-21 days) between the darkening of the sun and the actual return of Christ. An unbiased reading of the passage does not suggest such an interval of time and neither do the compan-ion passages in the Synoptic Gospels, especially Matthew 24:29-30. An appropriate reading of the text reveals that the darkening of the sun and other cataclysmic events *immediately* usher in the return of Christ on the clouds, not precede Him by weeks of time. In addition, Camping does not cite any Scripture that vali-dates a 9 to 21 day interval. It appears once again that Camping is reading into the text something he would like to see, or has to see, to make his end-time theory pan out (p. 526-527).

In the past, Camping often faulted the pre-Tribulation rapturists because they believed there was seven years between the rapture of the Church and the second coming of Christ. Camp-ing based his critique on the precise language of Matthew 24:29-30 which states: "Immediately after the tribulation of those days, the sun shall be darkened. . . . At that time the sign of the Son of Man will appear. . . ." Camping claimed that the word "immedi-ately" negated any time interval between the end of the Tribula-tion and the Second Coming. Apparently, "immediately" is not so *immediate* any longer since Camping now says there are 9 to 21 days between these events.

It would be appropriate to point out here that the darkening of the sun for 9-21 days presents other practical and exegetical problems for Camping. First, any darkening of the sun for just a mere few days, such that it does not emit heat or light, would soon turn the earth into a frozen wasteland. Temperatures would quickly plummet to sub-zero levels killing most, if not all, life on earth. Heating devices would break down as fuel and water sources and mechanical parts become frozen. In this scenario, Christ would come back to a lifeless planet — a scene that the Scriptures do not portray. Second, in comparing Camping's interpretation of Matthew 24:29 with other passages that speak of a cataclysmic end to the universe, there are quite a few contradictions in his scenario. For example, 2 Peter 3:10-12 gives a picture of the total collapse of the universe as both the heavens and the earth are destroyed with intense heat. Surely no one could survive this destruction and be waiting for Christ to return in 9-21 days. Moreover, Revelation 6:12-17, whose language is almost identical with Matthew 24:29 as it speaks of the darkening of the sun and moon, the falling of the stars to earth, and the powers of the heavens shaken, (adding that the sky is rolled up like a scroll), a passage which Camping believes occurs at the *same time* as Matthew 24:29, does not suggest a one to three-week interlude during these cataclysmic events. In the midst of this collapse the men of the earth see the face of God as He sits on a throne and in fear they speak of the great "day," (not 9-21 days) of His wrath that has come. For Camping's scenario to be true, the heavenly bodies could be removed (sun, moon, and stars), the earth's atmosphere obliterated (the sky rolled up and the powers of the heavens shaken), and the remaining elements of the universe be destroyed (with intense heat), and yet there would still be human beings existing for 9-21 days anticipating Christ's return. This, to say the least, is a very unlikely sequence of events.

12

Distorting Daniel's Prophecies

by Robert Sungenis

Nowhere is the confusing switch between literal and spiritual interpretation more evident than in Camping's treatment of Daniel 9 and 12. (Please bear with me as this analysis becomes very tedious.) After spiritualizing the command to *"rebuild and restore Jerusalem"* as applying to the re-establishment of the "law" under Ezra in 458 B.C., Camping proposes two pathways of Daniel's seventy-sevens. The first is done by adding 490 years to 458 B.C. which equals A.D. 33, the year Camping proposes that Christ was crucified. In the second pathway Camping incorporates the Jewish Jubilee feasts upon which analysis he conveniently allows himself to subtract 3 years from the 490 years. The remaining 487 year period (69 weeks plus 1/2 of the seventieth week) then traverses from 458 B.C. till the crucifixion of Jesus in A.D. 33. Hence, the 69 weeks transpire to A.D. 29 and the first half of Daniel's seventieth week transpires from the fall of A.D. 29 till the spring of A.D. 33 (p. 391-402).

The second half of the seventieth week is where Camping must do even more fancy foot-work since he claims that it transpires from A.D. 33 until A.D. 1994. Camping realizes that this is a big pill to swallow since he has just used a very literal interpretation for the three previous verses of Daniel 9:24-26. Nevertheless he insists that it can work no other way (p. 403). Because these numbers must fit into his already developed numerical scheme, the switching from literal to spiritual years is completely justified in his mind. Hence, Camping concludes that though the first three and one half years are literal, the second three and one half years must be spiritualized into 1,961 years — the time span from A.D. 33 to A.D. 1994.

Camping is more or less forced to find a symbolic meaning to the 1,961 years between A.D. 33 and A.D. 1994, since he previously stated that the time span between A.D. 33 and A.D. 1988 is "highly significant" because it is a product of 5 x 23 x 17 (see chapter 11). If 1988 produced such significant numbers, surely we would expect that 1994 must do likewise since it is the *actual* end of the world. True to form, Camping finally squeezed out a symbolic meaning to the number 1,961 in his "Family Bible Study" of July 7, 1994. Camping purported that in 1,961 years, being a product of 37 x 53 was "very, very significant." As noted previously, Camping considers 37 to be symbolic of judgment (see chapter 6). However, the number 53 is not mentioned once in the Bible. Undaunted by this absence, Camping figured out a way to extract 53 from the Bible and give it symbolic meaning. He turned to 1 Chronicles 9:22 and discovered that there were 212 porters to the tabernacle gates. Since these porters were divided into four quarters, there were most likely 53 on each side. Almost magically, Camping has found his convincing evidence. He adds that since the porters let people in and out of the tabernacle, this is similar to the task of believers from A.D. 33 to A.D. 1994 who let people in and out of the Church through the gospel. Hence, 53 is found to be symbolic. This is certainly a contrived formulation, especially since the number 53 is not found anywhere in the Bible to support his theory. And, despite the fact that Camping claims that Satan was loosed and the true gospel was virtually silenced in 1988, he has no problem with saying that the letting "in and out through the gospel" can take place until 1994. Once again we see that when one allows himself to spiritualize the text at will, he can twist almost any fact and make it fit into his preconceived ideas.

Another case of alternating between literal and spiritual interpretation to make the numbers fit is evidenced in Daniel 12. In verse 7, Daniel speaks of a *"time, time and half-time"* which Camping relates to the 42 months, 1,260 days, or time, time and half-time in Revelation 11-13. This period is spiritualized into the time span from the Cross till the end of the world. Next, in Daniel 12:11, Camping says that the 1,290 days are actually 1,290 years (similar to when Camping turned the 390 days of Ezekiel 4:5 into 3,900 years). Rather than point them to the future as he did with the 1,260 days, the 1,290 year period is said to refer to the past transpiring from 1877 B.C. to 587 B.C. The date of 1877 B.C. is said to be the starting point since it is the year that Israel entered Egypt. The date of 587 B.C. is said to be the ending point since it was the time when the Babylonians finally conquered Judah. Camping then introduces the two events of Daniel 12:11, that is, 1) the taking away of the *"daily"* (or *"candlestick"*) and, 2) the setting up of the abomination of desolation, and says that they describe the 1,290 year period from 1877 B.C. to 587 B.C. Thus, 1877 B.C. becomes the date when the *"daily"* is taken away, and 587 B.C. becomes the date when the *"abomination of desolation"* is set up. Here we have an odd combination of literal and spiritual interpretation of time spans within the same context, along with making a *prophecy* point to the past.

To impress us with more intricate numerical calculations, Camping also tells us that the 1,290 years, if multiplied by 3, equals 3,870 years, which if added to the original starting point of 1877 B.C. brings us exactly to 1994. Thus, we are led to believe that the already spiritualized 1,290 years can be re-spiritualized by a factor of 3 and take us to the supposed date of the end of the world. Camping would tell us that this calculation is completely legitimate because "3" represents the "purpose of God" and it is God's purpose to bring an end to the world. Of course, it is not hard to surmise that if the world were to end in A.D. 3284 Camping would tell us that this would be totally appropriate since the number "4" [(1,290 x 4) + 1,877 = 3,284] represents the "universality" of God's judgment at the end of the world. Any number can be made to fit into the theory if one can use broad categories of meaning.

Next, Camping comes to the 1,335 days of Daniel 12:12.

Apparently, he cannot make this number fit either historically or spiritually within the time frame of either the 1,260 days or the 1,290 days. Thus, Camping hypothesizes that the *"he"* of the phrase *"blessed is he who comes to the 1,335 day"* refers to Christ. This allows him to take the passage out of the historical context and place it in a time and location more to his liking. Camping then makes an elaborate calculation (whose addition is forced and inaccurate) from the baptism of Christ in the fall of A.D. 29 to the spring of A.D. 33 when Pentecost occurred, showing us that, opposed to the spiritualized 1,260 and 1,290 days, this is a very literal 1,335 days (p. 408-410).

As noted previously, one of the main reasons Camping can make his numbers fit so precisely is that he chooses his own beginning and ending points. The immediate context of Daniel 12:11-12 where the 1,335 days is found specifies that the beginning point of this period is when the daily sacrifice is taken away and the ending point is 45 days after the abomination of desolation is set up. Camping totally ignores this context. Then, when he begins calculating, he allows himself to manipulate his own beginning point by appealing to extra-biblical Jewish records that apparently allowed certain days to be shifted in the calendar by as much as two days. Camping conveniently uses one of these two days so that he can arrive at 1,335 days instead of 1,334 days. Nowhere does the Bible support such manipulation of dates and contexts.

After reading this novel exegesis, one again wonders what limits there are to such a subjective hermeneutic. Camping has arbitrarily switched from spiritual to literal interpretation, and back again, as well as employed three totally different epochs of the historical record as boundary points for Daniel's time periods. Ironically, it was Camping himself who said that numerical schemes must be supported by the Bible (p. 382). A natural reading of the context of Daniel 12 does not lend itself to this type of anachronistic and arbitrary exegesis. The setting of Daniel 12 places all these occurrences within the same chronological proximity. It is totally out of context to suggest that the *"taking away of the daily"* in Daniel 12:11 has any reference to the entrance of the Israelites into Egypt that happened over a thousand years earlier. Besides, even Camping's spiritualized interpretation of the *"taking away of the daily"* as a sign of ultimate apostasy does not coincide with the biblical account of Israel's stay in Egypt. The biblical record states that the Jews continued to multiply, worship God, and sacrifice in the land of Goshen, undisturbed and blessed for many years. They were not "apostate" as Camping's theory of the 1,290 days must claim. Rather, they were under God's guiding hand, soon to be delivered from their enemies.

In addition, it is a contradiction to say that the abomination of desolation ends, on the one hand, in 587 B.C. at the START of a 70-year "tribulation" period during the Babylonian captivity, but spiritually ENDS at A.D. 1994 when the "Tribulation" period has supposedly already expired because Christ has returned. It is interesting to note that Camping had previously alerted us to the fact that there were exactly 13,000 years between the creation date of 11013 B.C. and the beginning of the Tribulation period in 1988. It would seem, however, that even in Camping's scheme of things, the ending of his 3,870 years (1290 x 3) should be the beginning (1988), rather than the end (1994), of the Tribulation period since the original reference to his 1,290 years in Daniel 12:11 coincides with the beginning of the abomination of desolation, i.e., "tribulation." Similarly, the 13,000 years should point directly to the end of time (1994), rather than the beginning of Camping's Tribulation period (1988), since there is really no spiritual relationship between the creation and the setting up of the abomination of desolation.

Camping also does not explain how there can be 2,300 days between the taking away of the daily and the subsequent desolation of Daniel 8:13-14, but 1,290 days between the same events in Daniel 12:11 or 11:31. In addition, Camping offers no exegesis of Daniel 11 with its complicated and detailed conflict of Middle East nations that, according to Daniel 12:1, takes place at the same time as Daniel 12. Probably the main reason for Camping's silence on Daniel 11 is that its many and intricate details of future events, found nowhere else in the Bible, make it extremely difficult for him to match up the chapter with his interpretations of the remainder of Daniel and the Book of Revelation. Since Camping has fixated on a 1994 date for the return of Christ, it seems that anything that does not lend itself to that date is either spiritualized to make it fit or it is ignored as is Daniel 11. The closest Camping comes to exegeting Daniel 11 is to say that the "king of the north" refers to the kingdom of Satan whereas the "king of the south" refers to the New Testament external Church. These are two of Camping's most common answers when he confronts narrative items with a high degree of polarity. Broad spiritual categories are assigned so that the margin of error is minimized.

13

Discrediting Long-Held Interpretations for One's Own Interpretation

by Robert Sungenis

One of the passages that Camping uses to bolster his end-time scheme of dating is his unique interpretation of Matthew 24. Asserting that theologians of the past were all in error since they were looking for physical fulfillments of Matthew's prophecy, Camping claims to come to the rescue by proposing a decidedly spiritual interpretation of the passage, though, even he is not consistent to this premise. Camping dogmatically proclaims that any interpretation of Matthew 24 that purports to be fulfilled in the destruction of Jerusalem by the Romans in A.D. 70 is totally invalid.

At the outset we must admit that the interpretation of Matthew 24 is an exercise not without difficulties. The history of interpretation regarding Matthew 24 gives great evidence to this challenge. Some see the chapter applying only to the destruction of Jerusalem in A.D. 70 while others see not only that destruction but also clear references to the second coming of Christ. Where most exegetes have not been so dogmatic, Camping has claimed to have the definitive answer to Matthew 24. His is an entirely unique interpretation. To my knowledge, no theologian has ever seen Matthew 24 quite like Camping. He departs from the rest of the field by purporting that *all* of Matthew 24 is speaking of the events surrounding the second coming of Christ. In order to reach such a conclusion, Camping has to put his spiritualizing hermeneutic in high gear. Since the chapter includes such obvious references to first century Jewish items as "the temple" (verse 1), "the holy place" (verse 15), "Judea" (verse 16), "the Sabbath" (verse 20), not to mention the items in the companion passage of Luke 21:5-24 such as "the synagogues" (verse 12) and "Jerusalem surrounded by armies" (verse 20), Camping must assign a spiritualized meaning to each of these items in order to make them fit into our contemporary setting. To all other interpreters these particular items are obvious clues that at least the major part of the chapter is dealing with the first-century Jewish people, but not Camping. As with his other interpretations, Camping esteems his break with the ranks as evidence that God has blessed only him with the truth.

As always, it is interesting to see the exegetical contortions in which Camping engages to spiritualize verses in order to make them fit into his overall scheme of things. Regarding the reference to "the temple" and the surrounding structures Camping says that these cannot refer to the literal buildings in Jerusalem because Jesus said *"not one stone shall be left upon another."* Camping concludes that he could not have been referring to the temple buildings of Jerusalem, since in Jerusalem today one can still see the wailing wall which is made of stones, one on top of the other. Note here that Camping chooses to be very literal with biblical language when it suits his purpose. If Jesus says "not one stone" obviously it means no stones are standing. Since it was not fulfilled literally, Camping says it must be interpreted spiritually. Camping's alternative interpretation contends that the temple is a symbol of the New Testament church in which each believer is a *stone.* Because such passages as 1 Peter 2:5 use the metaphor of "living stones " to refer to Christians, Camping feels perfectly justified in injecting this metaphor back into Matthew 24:1-2. When Jesus says the stones will be cast down, Camping says that this refers to the Tribulation period when Christians (i.e., stones) are forced out of their churches (i.e., temples) due to false doctrine. As we will see in chapter 14, this is typical of Camping's overheated use of his Bible concordance such that if he finds one instance in which a particular word is used symbolically, he reserves to himself the right to use that symbolism in any other verse he chooses. However, in spiritualizing the text so flagrantly, many times the symbols come back to haunt the interpreter.

For instance, Camping believes that not all Christians have been forced from their churches today. In fact, he believes there are still people being saved in these churches. If Camping says that these Christians are stones, how can this be reconciled with his previous analysis that there would be *"not one stone left standing in the temple?"* If symbolically there are not stones left in the temple, then for Camping there can be no Christians left in any of the churches of today, a conclusion he would not admit. Camping can be very literal when it is his objective to critique other exegetes, but not very literal when he is formulating his own interpretation.

In turn, Camping also spiritualizes the reference to the *"holy place"* and the *"fleeing from Judea to the mountains"* in Matthew 24:15-16 which both become symbols of those who must flee the apostate New Testament external Church that will have been overrun by false gospels. Next, the *"tribulation"* in verse 21, though it is given a literal time period to transpire from other texts (i.e., 2300 days), is said to have nothing to do with literal trauma or bloodshed. Like most of his end-time figures, it is spiritualized to refer to a time when hardly anyone is receiving salvation. *"Those who give suck,"* and whose *"flight may be on the sabbath or in winter"* in verses 19-20 are not given a detailed explanation by Camping except that "winter" symbolically refers to a time of very little salvation (p. 227). From other studies, Camping says the sabbath refers to people who try to work for their salvation. Again, these interpretations are not derived from a natural reading of the text but are contrived due to the presuppostions Camping has cemeted in his mind before ever coming to the text. These kinds of interpretations are prime examples which show the lengths Camping will go to make the text fit into his preconceived ideas.

A few years ago, Camping understood the phrase, "woe to those who give suck" as referring either to children born from unsaved familes in the Tribulation period who could not receive salvation because the gospel had been silenced and/or that God would close the wombs of Christian women so they could no longer bear children. He has since retracted both these interpetations due, in part, to the fact that many of his followers were continuing to have children after 1988. Camping now believes that the phrase refers to parents who guide their children into apostasy. Also, Camping has recently concluded that the phrase "pray that your flight be not in winter" was a prayer that could legitimately be prayed by all Christians prior to 1988. The prayer was to ask God to spare them from going through the Tribulation (i.e., "winter"). If they prayed to die and were deceased before 1988, their prayer was answered. Those Christians existing after 1988 can no longer pray to escape the Tribulation by the simple fact that they are already in it. These reinterpretations were made in a recent "Family Bible Study" program. These views show that when one consistently spiritualizes the biblical text he eventually paints himself into a theological corner and the only escape is to make absurd hypotheses like the one above concerning how God answers prayer.

Camping presumes that all of Matthew 24 must refer to the end of the world since in the opening question the Apostles ask when Christ's *"coming"* will be and when the *"end of the world"* will occur. Though these terms may be used in different texts to refer to the final appearance of Christ at the end of time, this by no means precludes that they can refer to a time prior to the final consumation. Though the phrase "end of the world" is found in some translations, such as the King James Version, it is not an exact rendering of the Greek. It is more correctly read as, *"the end of the age."* Matthew chose to use the Greek word "aionos" ("age") which refers to a period of time rather than "kosmos" ("world").

There are two main "ages" that the Bible uses to divide the present time. The age of the Jews, commonly known as the Old Testament, and the age of the Church, commonly known as the New Testament. When the latter age came, the former age was replaced. It is one of the major themes in the Bible. During Jesus'

Olivet discourse, the age of the Old Testament is coming to a close. After hearing Jesus make some remarkable statements here and in Matthew 23 condemning the Jews and predicting the demise of Jerusalem, the Apostles become curious as to when this destruction will occur. It is a natural question to ask when we consider that Jesus just told them that the Jewish temple would be destroyed. Perhaps the Apostles thought that the end of the age of Judaism would also be the end of the world and the final appearance of Jesus as even others are said to have believed (2 Thess. 2:1). As some have suggested, perhaps Jesus is answering two questions, one concerning the destruction of Jerusalem the other concerning His second coming. If so, the Apostles didn't realize, nor did Jesus specify, that there would be thousands of years between these two events.

Regarding the *"coming"* of Jesus of which the Apostles inquired, this does not have to be confined to Christ's final coming at the end of time. Indeed, after his resurrection Jesus made several "comings" in one form or another in order to establish His kingdom (Acts 2:20; 7:55; 9:4-5; 10:13-15; 22:17-18; 23:11; Rev. 1:7). Similarly, Jesus told the Apostles in Matthew 16:27-28 that some of them would not die until they saw the Son of Man *"coming in his kingdom."* (The same Greek word "erchomenos" [coming] is used in Matthew 24:30, 44; Luke 18:18; 21:27 in reference to Christ's coming.) Since the "kingdom" was not necessarily something that would only be fulfilled at the end of time (Matt. 10:7, 23; 12:28; Luke 11:20) then it is perfectly valid to search for the coming of the Kingdom before that time. In fact, since the quick and sudden appearance of the Kingdom might not have been easily understood or believed possible, Jesus introduces the fact with marked solemnity in the statement, "Truly I say unto you" in order to impress His imminent coming on their minds. Camping holds that the transfiguration in Matthew 17:1 was the fulfillment of the coming Kingdom in Matthew 16:28. This cannot be correct since none of the Apostles died before that event had occurred just six days later. Jesus was clear that only "some" (Greek plural: "tines") of the Apostles would be living when Matthew 16:28 was fulfilled.

Perhaps Pentecost could be a fulfillment (see Acts 2:20) but only one Apostle, Judas , had died by then. There was only one coming of Christ in which a plurality of the Apostles would have already died leaving only *"some"* still living. Only the coming of Christ in judgment upon Israel in A.D. 70 can fulfill the requirements of Matthew 16:28. When the temple was destroyed this was the "sign" that Jesus had finally "come" and visited the long-awaited judgment upon Jerusalem. The destruction of the temple was, indeed, the final blow to the age of Judaism, culminating with the generation of Jews in Jesus' day. It was one of their greatest tragedies, their *"great tribulation,"* as it were, that they would ever experience. In that generation they would cease to exist as a nation and finally have the custody of the Word of God taken away from them. The Pharisees certainly knew that Jesus was speaking personally of the impending destuction, and that is precisely why they wanted to kill Him (Matt. 21:43-45; 23:36).

Regarding the statement in Matthew 24:14 that the gospel would be preached to the whole world before the end would come, this also does not have to be addressing the years immediately before the end of time. Passages such as Colossians 1:6 and 23 specify that from the perspective of the New Testament the gospel had already been preached to the "whole world" during Paul's time. Indeed, historical records show that the gospel was preached to the whole inhabited world within 40 years of Jesus' ascension. Being already an accomplished fact from the perspective of the New Testament, today's succession of gospel preaching cannot be used as a criterion to chart the timing of the end of the world.

Regarding the language describing the disruption of the heavenly bodies in Matthew 24:29, though there may be some prophetic tie-in to the actual obliteration of the sun, moon, and stars at the end of time, this type of language is by no means confined by the Bible to end-time events. The Bible is replete with identical references concerning the cataclysm of the heavenly bodies whenever a major judgment of God was coming upon a particular nation (Isaiah 13:9-10 against Babylon; Isaiah 34:4-5 against Edom; Ezekiel 32:7-8 against Egypt; Amos 5:18; 8:9 against Israel).

Though one could make a case that these descriptions could also telescope into the collapse of the universe at the end of time, this cannot take away from the fact that these solar upheavals are metaphorically applied to the time in which the prophet was writing without the least bit of anachronism. The same can be said for the blowing of the trumpet and the sending of the angels to gather the elect (Isa. 27:13; Deut. 30:4; Zech. 2:6). We must understand that the phophets often used global and/or catastrophic language even thought they may have only been referring to one particular time and place in the world. Jesus is simply following in the same prophetic genre.

Regarding the reference to *"this generation"* in Matthew 24:34, though there are passages in the Old Testament that may indicate a wider range of meaning for the phrase (Ps. 24:6), the preponderant use of "this generation" refers to the actual generation of people existing at a certain point in history. Moreover, one cannot take the contextual meaning of a word from one place and automatically assume the same meaning exists for a different context in which the word is used.

To support his thesis that all of Matthew 24 centers around the second coming of Christ, Camping asserts that "this generation" can only refer to the "generation of evil." He cites, for example, Luke 11:50 in which Jesus said that the judgment for the murders of the prophets from Abel to Zechariah would come upon "this generation." If, as Camping critiques, "this generation" refers only to the Jews of the first century, then this would be unfair of God to punish the Jews living in the first century for the crimes of Jews long ago. What Camping fails to understand is that God often visited the iniquity of the fathers upon the children (Exod. 20:4; Jer. 32:18). When the Jews were taken into the Assyrian and Babylonian captivities, the generation that went captive were paying for their sins as well as the sins of their forefathers that God tolerated for so long. God had finally given up on them.

In the case of the Jew of Jesus' day, they added tremendously to the sins of their fathers who persecuted the prophets, for persecuting Christ was the ultimate blasphemy. In fact, following His harshest tirade, Jesus tells them in Matthew 23:32, *"Fill up, then, the measure of the sins of your forefathers."* Here Jesus specifies the intimate connection between the sins of the fathers and their progeny. As Paul says of them: *". . . who killed the Lord Jesus and the prophets, and also drove us out . . . in this way they always heap up their sins to the limit. The wrath of God has come upon them fully"* (1 Thess. 2:15-16). The "heaping up" of sins over a period of time is what brings God's ultimate judgment. The Jews of Jesus' day were finishing the sins of their fathers who began the rejection of God by persecuting and killing those from Abel to Zechariah. They are the generation who receive the final and most severe judgment of God.

Other instances in which it is clear that *"this generation"* refers to the contemporaries of that day include Matthew 11:16-24 and 12:41. In the first reference, speaking to the unbelieving Jews of His day Jesus remarks on the manner that *"this generation"* has responded to the message of God. He indicates that they rejected both John the Baptist and himself. Since both John and Jesus existed only in the time of that particular generation of Jews, naturally the phrase *"this generation"* refers only to those specific Jews.

In additon, Jesus also rebukes the Jewish cities of Chorazin and Bethsaida, contrasting their unrepentance with those long ago in Tyre and Sidon who would have repented had they received the same warning. Chorazin and Bethsaida were cities in the generation of Jews in the first century. Jesus was not referring to all the "generation of evil" before the existence of Chorazin and Bethsaida. Finally, in Matthew 12:41, Jesus speaks of the men of Ninevah (circa 800 B.C.) who will stand up at judgment day to condemn "this generation" of Jews. Although the Ninevites repented within *40 days* of hearing Jonah's voice, we know the Jews of Jesus' day would not repent within *40 years* of hearing Christ's voice, a voice far greater than Jonah's. Again, the contrast is between two specific groups of people — the Ninevites and the Jews of Jesus' day, not the whole human race of evil men.

One reason Camping discounts the A.D. 70 interpretation is that the New Testament does not document the literal destruction of Jerusalem. However, there is no hermeneutical rule that requires specific New Testament documentation of the destruction of Jerusalem in order for it to be applicable to Matthew 24 anymore than it is required when Camping, for example, claims that Christ was born in 7 B.C. without specific New Testament documentaion. But for the sake of argument, the New Testament contains sufficient information pointing to the Roman armies. For example, Luke 19:41-44 gives us the first hint that an army would destroy Jerusalem, precisely the way history tells us that the Romans encircled the city, in the years immediately following Jesus' remarks. Similarly, John 11:48 specifies that the Jews were fully aware that the Romans could come and destroy their holy place and nation. Camping, as would be expected, spiritualizes the clear language of Luke 19:41-44, ascribing it to the "end-time apostate external Church" that is "surrounded by the armies of Satan." He also spiritualizes the language of Luke 21:20-24 which specifies a clear distinction between Jews and Gentiles.

To understand more fully why the destruction of Jerusalem and the downfall of Judaistic religion is such a pivotal event in understanding the events of Matthew 24 one need only to read the Acts of the Apostles or the epistles of Paul. In these books, Peter, Paul, and the other Apostles and elders are viciously slandered and attacked by the fanatical Jews of that day. Indeed, in almost every chapter of the Book of Acts the Jews were antagonizing the Christians (Acts 2:13; 4:1; 5:17; 6:8; 7:54; 8:1; 9:22; 12:1; 13:6, 45; 14:2; 17:5, 13; 18:6, 28; 19:9; 20:3, 19; 21:11, 27; 22:22; 23:1; 24:5; 25:7; 26:2). Similarly, in the Epistles, the Judaizers were one of the Apostles' most formidable opponents to the new Christian faith (2 Cor. 11:24; Gal. 2:13; 3:1; 5:22; Col. 2:16; 1 Thess. 2:14; Rev. 2:9; 3:9).

With all this evidence of the Jewish persecution of the Church through much of the first century, the question would naturally surface as to how long God was going to let this go on. When would the Jews be punished and set aside so that Christianity could flourish? In God's wisdom, He used the persecution from the Jews to help spread the Christian faith beyond the borders of Jerusalem (Acts 8:1; 11:19; 14:6). After Christianity had spread over the whole inhabited world, God no longer needed the goad of Judaism and thus lowered His judgment against the Jews in A.D. 70.

Though, as mentioned previously, there may be a telescoping of some of the events of Matthew 24 to the actual end of the world, we can safely say that any interpretation that does not incorporate the destruction of Jerusalem in A.D. 70 is ignoring some of the most fundamental principles of biblical interpretation, the most vivid historical precedent available, and the witness from two millenia of Christian exegets. In Camping's "all or nothing, black and white" approach to the Scriptures, his spiritualizing form of interpretation seems to be the most important things for him to preserve. Once he spiritualizes one part of the text, his self-imposed hermeneutic forces him to do likewise with the rest of the text. As a result, the passage is severely distorted and emptied of its historical meaning and fulfillment. In the next chapter we well see much more evidence of the damage Camping's esoteric exegesis has caused.

14

Forming One's Own Rules for Biblical Interpretation
by Robert Sungenis

As evidenced throughout this critique, much of Camping's hermeneutic consists of spiritualizing the Scripture. It cannot be understated that Camping is convinced that he has been given the key to unlock the mysteries of the Bible by the use of the spiritualizing method of interpretation. In using what he calls "word studies," a particular word of a verse is compared to its other usages in the Bible before an exegesis is made. A definition is formulated and injected back into the verse in question. Though word studies, when used properly, are a useful tool in biblical interpretation, Camping's word studies are a unique combination of subjectivism and symbolism that usually distort the passage instead of making it clearer. Claiming that he is only releasing the gospel message latent within every page of the Bible, Camping's "word studies" often make verses of Scripture say something totally different than what they were meant to say. In chapter two we have already seen how his word studies have distorted the meaning of the phrase "day and hour" in Mark 13:32, but more evidence is available to show the frequent misinterpretations and hidden agendas common in this type of hermeneutic.

Erroneous Interpretations at Family Radio

During my stay at Family Radio, I wrote many booklets on various Christian topics for our correspondence students. The last three, which eventually led to my dismissal from Family Radio, included: the use of wine, divorce and remarriage, and biblical interpretation. When I first came to Family Radio, Camping and I were in agreement on these topics. But as I began to delve deeper into the interpretive presuppositions behind these beliefs, I knew something was amiss at Family Radio. I tried my best to show the errors we were making but Camping turned a deaf ear and actually became more adamant about his stance. The following are some of the many confrontations we had.

In the book *1994?* Camping states: *"We must never force a statement of the Bible so that we can understand it to say what it has not said"* (p. 26). Though Camping constantly accuses others of "forcing" conclusions from the Bible, he is one of the biggest offenders of this practice. For example, in our discussions on the use of wine, Camping, being a devout teetotaler, emptied the Bible of any suggestion that a Christian could drink wine. In his interpretation of 1 Timothy 3:8, for example, which states that "a deacon shall not be given to much wine" (KJV), Camping, did his best to rid the verse of the suggestion that a deacon can drink *some* wine. Regardless of one's personal view on whether alcoholic beverages are proper for Christians, the important point to notice here is how Camping arrived at his position. He formed his belief by an analysis of the word *"much,"* discovering in his concordance another usage in John 12:24 where Jesus, speaking metaphorically of himself and Christians, uses the analogy that a grain of corn must die and bear *"much"* fruit. Completing his word study, Camping proposed that since Christ's work in Christians is perfect, they will bear *"all"* fruit, not just *"much"* fruit. He then concluded that "much" can mean "all." This altered definition of "much" was then transferred back into 1 Timothy 3:8 to read, "a deacon shall not be given to *all* (or *any*) wine." From this analysis Camping insisted that neither deacons, nor anyone else, could drink wine for pleasure. As a result, the book I had written on the use of wine was severely altered by Camping before its publication.

Camping and I had our biggest bout over the interpretation of Matthew 19:9 where Jesus says, "Whosoever divorces his wife, except for fornication, and marries another, commits adultery." Since Camping believed his Protestant brethren who used this verse to allow divorce for fornication were wrong, he did his best to change the meaning of the exception clause. He supported this contention by a word study on *"except,"* finding another usage in Matthew 19:17 where Jesus says, "there is none good except God." Camping proposed that the Greek word "ei mee," ("except"), could be translated as *"in addition to"* so that the sentence could read, "there is none good in addition to God" and mean exactly the same thing as when using the word *"except."*[1] This is certainly true, but what he didn't tell his audience was that in the English language the negative word *"none"* makes the phrase *"in addition to"* a negative statement, forcing it to subtract from a stated proposition, the same subtraction that the word *"except"* performs. Camping then took the meaning of *"none . . . in addition to"* that subtracted from the stated proposition in Matthew 19:17, secretly eliminated the word *"none,"* and put the remaining phrase, *"in addition to,"* back into Matthew 19:9, *but still kept the meaning that subtracts from a stated proposition.* Hence, the verse was made to read: "Whosoever divorces his wife, 'in addition to' fornication, and marries another, commits adultery." By this sleight of hand "word study," Camping made the verse say exactly the opposite of what it was intended to say. In Camping's mind, fornication was now an *additional reason* one could not separate from his wife. Despite my repeated attempts at revealing this blatant error to Camping, he continually ignored my pleas and accused me of sanctioning divorce. To no avail, I tried to assure him that I was against divorce just as much as he was, but I was equally interested in not distorting the biblical language just to prove a point.

These kinds of distortions are a symptom of a much larger problem in the hermeneutic of Harold Camping. To boil his exegetical method down to its basic components, Camping believes that words in the Bible can only be defined by comparing them with other biblical words, not by their lexical or grammatical meaning:

If we wish to know the meaning of a word in the Bible, we do not go to a dictionary of Greek or Hebrew (the original languages of the Bible). To do so would be useless. The meanings of words have changed during the last 2,000 years. Ideally, the rules of grammar and the meanings of words should be derived entirely from the Bible, because the Bible alone must be the final authority in all matters of which it speaks (AYR: p. 76, 78).

Hence, a word may have a very technical meaning in Greek but Camping reserves himself the right to ignore this definition because, he claims, *"the Bible is its own dictionary."* By making such a dichotomy between the lexical meaning and the "biblical" meaning, not only does Camping wrench the Bible from its grammatical/historical milieu, but he creates a very self-serving hermeneutic since then he can make the words of the Bible mean virtually anything he wants, which he often does. The definition of biblical words become totally dependent on one's subjective interpretation of the passage in which the word is contained.

As far as answering the anomaly of biblically defining words used only once in the Bible (known as "hapax legomena"), Camping says: "In this case it cannot be compared with its use in other parts of the Bible. However, we can be sure that the *content* of the word will convey a truth that is found in other parts of the Bible. . . . It is best to leave it in its original language and trust that at a future date God will open the eyes of a Bible student to learn its meaning"(emphasis mine).[2]

First, how can one determine the content of a word if he cannot be sure which other biblical words he should compare it? At some point Camping must rely on the lexical meaning to make an initial matchup. Second, how is God going to reveal this knowledge, if, as Camping has repeatedly claimed, God will not communicate to us outside the Bible? Consequently, it remains that Camping does not have an adequate answer for words used once in the Bible and thus there is a major discrepancy in his theory on how biblical words are to be defined. Though the Bible may put one slant or another on the lexical meaning of a Greek word, it does not alter the lexical meaning. Nowhere does the Bible claim such a preroga-tive for itself, and words used once in the Bible prove this.

Though Camping does not readily admit or expound on this fact due to the ramifications it would have, he believes that God specifically reveals interpretations of the Bible to him. This is the major reason Camping feels that he understands end-time prophecies better than anyone else. Are these clear and distinct revelations without doubt or confusion? Camping does not elabo-rate. If he did claim they were clear and distinct he would cer-tainly run the risk of not being able to distinguish between his private revelations from God and those of others who he vehe-mently condemns for receiving divine revelations outside the Bible.

To show the extent to which Camping believes God guides his thinking, he now believes that the statements in Mark 13:11 and Luke 21:14-15 (in which Jesus says not to be anxious what you will speak because the Holy Spirit will speak for you) apply not to the apostolic age only, but to the whole New Testament period, especially near the end of time ("Family Bible Study," March 1, 1993). Camping conveniently blurs the distinction be-tween the inspiration of the Holy Spirit and the proclamations of an uninspired spiritual man.

Along with his "word studies," Camping has another very effective method to make his interpretations appear to be correct and make the interpretations of others, that are equally as plau-sible, seem totally fallacious. Often when someone defends a doctrine that is taught in various verses of the Bible, Camping, seeing the force of these verses yet disagreeing with the pro-posed doctrine of the other person, will claim that the particular verses the person is citing must be interpreted "*in light of the rest of the Bible.* " Though comparing Scripture with Scripture is cer-tainly an excellent interpretive tool, often it is not what Camping practices. Camping will merely amass a string of verses that say the opposite of the other person's verses, and thereby claim that he (Camping) has used the *"whole"* Bible in his interpretation. Because Camping couches his conclusions in this way, he makes it seem as if the other person has ignored much of what the Bible has to say whereas only he (Camping) has been very faithful by using *"all"* of the Bible. But what is really happening is that

Camping sets up his favorite verses as the standard by which all other verses must be judged. As a result, he makes his verses *overrule* the other person's verses. Rather than finding a balance or synthesis between the conflicting verses, Camping invariably comes down on the side of the verses he likes best — those that fit with his theological perspective. Camping has not really consulted or reasoned with the whole Bible, rather, he long ago decided which verses he would like to see hold more weight and thus he continually uses them to neutralize other verses that say something different than what he prefers to believe. To the uneducated Bible student it appears as if Camping has really done his homework and the other person is made to look quite foolish. In reality, it is Camping who often gives the shoddy exegesis and ignores much of what the Bible has to say.

Many examples of Camping's biased exegesis of Scripture have already been cited, but another verse that Camping has consistently used to foster his brand of salvation is Romans 3:10-11 (p. 148). Camping extracts this verse and concludes that no men seek after God. But when this verse is compared to the passage from which it is quoted (Ps. 14), it can readily be seen that Camping's conclusion is totally incorrect. Psalm 14:1-3 certainly speaks of those who have turned aside and do not seek after God, but the verses immediately following in Psalm 14:4-7, a context with which the apostle Paul was certainly aware, makes a marked distinction between the "evildoers" who do not seek God and "my people," "the righteous," and the "poor" who have sought God and are oppressed by the evildoers. Similarly, Paul states in Acts 17:27 and 34 that God's pre-determinations are made precisely "so that men would seek him and perhaps reach out for him and find him . . . because he now commands all men everywhere to repent."

As for biblical languages, when it is to his advantage, Camping is quick to commandeer the Greek language for support. For example, in his exegesis of Romans 11:26 in *1994?* Camping harps on the error of the premillennialists who translate the Greek adverb *"houtos"* as *"then"* instead of *"so"* (p. 539). Camping has castigated these interpreters for years because they ignored the exact meaning of *"houtos."* Though in this instance Camping has stumbled onto the lexical meaning, he would claim that he is actually abiding by the "biblical" meaning of *"houtos."* By "biblical" he means that when he looked up all the ways his King James Bible translated *"houtos,"* it never translated it as "so," thus, it cannot mean "so." What Camping fails to understand is that the King James translators could not translate *"houtos"* as *"so"* because the *lexical* meaning of *"houtos"* in Greek would not allow such a definition, not because they gave preference to the "biblical" definition of the word. The disregard or ignorance of the Greek language, coupled with a distorted concept of how we received the Bible and its translations, consistently leads Camping to form these erroneous conclusions about the Bible's words and is the main reason he sees nothing wrong with altering the lexical meaning with his "word studies." By the same token, one wonders why Camping does not give the premillennialists license to alter the lexical definition of *"houtos"* based on how they feel the Bible is using the term.

At other times, Camping ignored the Greek altogether if it did not support his interpretation from the English. For example, in discussions we had at Family Radio of the King James Version of the phrase, *"the faith of Christ"* in Galatians 2:16, Camping insisted that this referred to "Christ's faith" rather than someone's "faith in Christ." He proceeded to make a major doctrine that a Christian is not saved by his faith in Christ but only by Christ's faith in God. I tried to point out to him that in the Greek there is a difference between an objective and subjective genitive of which Galatians 2:16 was the former. The objective genitive refers to *our* faith in Christ. Also, the next clause, *"and we have believed in Jesus Christ"* specified *our* faith. In addition, the King James Version of Galatians 3:26 used the Greek dative *"faith in Christ"* to clear up any ambiguity. Camping would hear none of this. He would never admit that the Greek could overrule his English interpretation, claiming instead that Greek grammar obtained its validity "only from the way the Bible used Greek words." Hence, since Camping had the last word on what the Bible was saying, he was the final judge of the meaning of the Greek and whether it could be used or not. If it supported him he used it, if it did not support him he ignored it.

As noted previously, Camping's most prized form of word study, and one that is consistently used in *1994?* is that which produces a "spiritual meaning." This is a word study that, unlike 1 Timothy 3:8, Matthew 19:9, or Galatians 2:16, in which the lexical meaning of a word or phrase is altered, spiritualizes the lexical meaning, as Camping claims, to give the message of the gospel in symbolic form. To the average Bible student, Camping's method seems very spiritual since most of his conclusions center around the gospel dimensions of salvation or judgment. To the trained observer, however, Camping often goes beyond the simple message of the Bible, distorting it in order to propel his own version of the gospel.

Camping reserves the right to interpret the Bible by spiritualized word studies because Mark 4:34 states that Jesus did not teach the people without a parable. We are constantly reminded by Camping that parables were given to hide the truth in symbolic language.[3] In Camping's mind, since Jesus speaks to us in the *whole Bible*, ipso facto, the whole Bible is a parable that must be unlocked of its secret meaning in order to get to the real truth (AYR: p. 101). Camping claims that only the spiritually discerning believer can see these hidden symbolic meanings. In turn, he consistently uses this hermeneutic as a spiritual club to knock down any other group that disagrees with him, claiming that they simply have not been given the proper tools by God to understand the Bible. The presumptuous view that the *whole Bible* is in parabolic language illustrates well the tendency Camping has of making the part equal to the whole, and then forming dogmatic conclusions on the whole he has created.

The result of this tendency is that if Camping finds just one instance in which a particular word is used "symbolically," he gives himself license to spiritualize any other usage of that word in the Bible. One example of Camping's spiritualized word studies which led to an interesting confrontation between us was his interpretation of Matthew 5:13 where Jesus states, *"you are the salt of the earth."* During my work at Family Radio, Camping's son-in-law, Tom Schaff, then manager of the short-wave department and fellow instructor at the school, had written a booklet entitled *Personal Bible Study*[4] which illustrated various techniques of biblical interpretation. In a few pages, Tom had outlined how one was to do a "word study," using the word *salt* as an example. First, Tom went back to Leviticus 2:13 in which the

Israelites were told to offer their sacrifices with salt. He then stated that these Old Testament sacrifices pointed to the sacrifice of Christ on the cross, at which time God poured out His judgment upon His Son. From this matchup, Tom wrote that whenever the word *"salt"* is used in the Bible it refers to God's judgment, hence, Matthew 5:13 really means, *"you are the judgment of the earth."* After reading this section, I quickly wrote Tom a letter explaining that this was not proper exegesis and offered a better solution that dealt with philological and contextual concepts. Apparently, Tom understood and agreed with what I said since during that same day I noticed him removing his booklets from the display case in the front lobby. Afterward, he presented his new learning to Camping, but within 24 hours the booklets were back on the display case. I knew from personal conversations with Camping that the interpretation had originated with him and he was not about to be undermined by any of his staff, especially his own son-in-law. Tom and I talked very little after that incident and I sensed that he was now commissioned by Camping to see what other evidence he could find of my "heretical" views.

Camping believes he must unlock these spiritual truths because "the gospel message is *hidden* in each historical event of the Bible." Though the Bible certainly uses types and anti-types to show the splendor of its message, Camping's self-imposed hermeneutic forces him to find a spiritual representation for every single person, place, or thing in a biblical narrative. After a while, the spiritualized meanings begin to overlap and subsequently conflict and contradict one another because there are just too many entities which need a spiritual meaning assigned to them but so few distinct spiritual truths to go around. Moreover, the real potential danger in the spiritualized interpretation of a historical narrative is that the interpretation will only be as good as one's understanding of the clear doctrinal propositions of Scripture. If one's doctrinal position is faulty he will just read these errors into the historical narrative that he spiritualizes and consequently he will exacerbate the doctrinal error. There are many such doctrinal errors that Camping reads into these historical narratives — his interpretation of "the faith of Christ" from Galatians 2:16, cited above, being one good example.

After listening to Camping's teaching for a while, one will notice that he seems to have an answer for virtually any question about the Bible that is posed to him. At times someone will call his "Open Forum" program and ask for an interpretation of some obscure Old Testament passage. It is obvious by Camping's hesitation that he does not always know what he is going to say. However, Camping will begin by rephrasing the caller's question into terms with which he feels more comfortable and then masterfully put together a detailed interpretation of the passage. The caller hangs up marveling how Camping seems to know so much of the Bible so quickly and readily. But what is really happening in many of these quick and ready answers is that Camping is thinking out the interpretation as he speaks. He begins by placing the various persons, places, and things of the passage into pre-packaged spiritual categories. The categories are simple positives and negatives: the kingdom of Christ or the kingdom of Satan, salvation or judgment, grace or works, good or evil, etc. After assigning a spiritual meaning to various aspects of the passage, Camping will interrelate them to one another and create the "gospel" message that the passage is supposedly portraying. It is a very simple process. The caller, not knowing any better, is very impressed with Camping and feels that he has finally found a "biblical" interpretation of the passage. In reality, he has just been indoctrinated with Camping's spiritualizing hermeneutic, not necessarily an accurate understanding of the passage at all.

Camping also sways the thinking of many naive Christians by first giving a very accurate and orthodox view of a certain Christian tenet. Once he has made an inroad and gained the listener's confidence, Camping will often veer off into his own ideas via the spiritualizing hermeneutic or word studies. The listener usually does not realize what is happening nor does he have the acumen to distinguish between the orthodox statements and the inventions of Camping. He thus assumes that all that he is hearing is biblical. In practical and moral theology much of what Camping teaches is correct. It is just the extra percentage that he adds of his own theology that causes such controversy.

One of the more repugnant interpretations created by Camping's word studies was the analysis of the word *"love"* in

1 Corinthians 13. Long honored as one of the most beautiful passages in Scripture, Camping's exegesis emptied the passage of its splendor and turned it into a sterile specimen of his own version of Christianity. Starting with the question, "What is love?" Camping claimed that because Paul chose a form of description that was negative, e.g., *"it does not envy, it does not boast, "* that he was not describing what love **was** but what it **was** not. This made room for Camping to insert his own definition of what love actually was. Doing a "word study" on love led Camping to the conclusion that love was simply preaching the gospel to the unsaved. He gave a similar interpretation to the command of Jesus to *"feed the hungry and clothe the naked"* in Matthew 25:31-46. Camping taught that this in no way referred to giving literal bread and clothing to needy people. That was purely a "social" gospel. Instead, it was turned into an exclusive command to preach the gospel of salvation and judgment. Naturally, this interpretation fit well with him since his whole ministry was centered around preaching Camping's version of the gospel over the air waves rather than helping people physically. This made him appear to exude love for his fellow man. Preaching the gospel is certainly one aspect of loving someone but as Paul says, "love *is eternal*," and as such, it involves many *virtuous qualities* that will continually be practiced in heaven long after gospel preaching has ceased. Taking care of the *whole* person is how Jesus extended His love, not just by "preaching."

There are many more predictions and numerical calculations within *1994?* that I could critique. The foregoing examples are sufficient to show the extreme distortions and self-serving agendas that can be produced by subjective "word studies" and "spiritual" perspectives. When one witnesses these flagrant distortions of the biblical text, he has to ask himself the fair question: *Is this the interpretive system I am going to trust to reveal the secrets of the Bible, especially the date of Christ's return?* After thoroughly reviewing *1994?* and *Are You Ready?* and other publications of Harold Camping, it becomes apparent that though he vigorously claims he is letting the Bible speak to him, in reality, Harold Camping often makes the Bible speak what he wants to hear. Hopefully, the examples cited in this book will suffice to show that Camping's spiritualizations and fancy numerical equations are simply an invention of his own mind. In using these convoluted methods to predict the end of the world, Camping may have fallen victim to his own warning:

> If a teacher or pastor declares to his congregation, "Thus saith the Lord," when the Lord has not said that, he is mouthing doctrines that are out of man's mind rather than God's. We immediately sense how reprehensible this is (AYR: p. 59).

In another light, though we must be very critical of those who attempt to date the end of the world, this is not to say that we cannot wonder if Christ will return soon. In times past, Christians have looked at the conditions of the world and wondered if Christ's return was imminent. Though possible, we just don't know if ours is the time. And there are very good and healthy reasons why God does not want us to know the date of His return. Besides, God has already built into each of us the knowledge that the end will come someday, either at death or the end of time. This knowledge is all that is needed. Though it is claimed that some may be influenced to turn to Christ if they knew the date of the end, in my experience, it causes more people to ridicule Christianity than believe in it due to the plethora of date setters in recent years that have all been wrong. Dating the end also causes much unnecessary anxiety in the daily decision-making among Christians. Unfortunately, I know some within the Family Radio circle who have already begun to sell their possessions, quit their jobs or schooling, load up their credit cards to make donations to Family Radio, and make other major decisions in their daily lives based on the fact that they don't expect the world to exist after September 1994.

Christ will come when He will come. Let us make sure that we are prepared for Him whenever He comes, be it next week or in the next millennium.

15

Predicting Christ's Return: The Dangers of Date Setting

David Allen Lewis

Bang-Ik Ha and his misguided Korean followers spent vast sums of money in 1992, announcing to the world that Jesus would rapture the Church on October 28, exactly at midnight. Large advertisements appeared in *USA Today* and other publications, telling that Jesus would come during the Feast of Trumpets and their *fyugo* (rapture) to heaven would take place.

A South African newspaper carried a Reuters report telling of adverse reaction in Korea: "Parent groups demand that the government act quickly for fear of mass suicides across the country if the predictions prove wrong." A Mr. Lee was quoted; "In outrage and despair, these believers, especially the young ones feeling betrayed, are very likely to end their lives blaming themselves."

The Reuters report added that South Korean prosecutors were probing complaints from parents alleging that these sects were abducting their children. When the whole thing failed on October 28, 1992, some of the preachers were attacked and even severely beaten by their enraged followers. There were reports of a few suicides. It was a tragedy.

In the nineteenth century, Rev. M. Baxter, an Anglican clergyman in England, identified Louis Napoleon as the Antichrist and predicted the battle of Armageddon for 1868. I have his rare, little, fragile pamphlet that speaks to me these words across the years, "Take warning! Learn not to repeat the errors of the past."

In the last century, Sir Robert Anderson, a fine scholar and great eschatologist, lamented, "And so in recent years, one date after another has been confidently named for the supreme crisis; but still the world goes on. A.D. 581 was one of the first years fixed for the event." Anderson was referring to the church father, Hippolytus, who said the end would come in the year 500.

Date setting is the curse of the Bible prophecy message and may prove to be more destructive than all external enemies put together. It is horrible to contemplate that a powerful biblical message may be eclipsed by the radical actions of the "friends of the message," but we sadly warn that this is what may happen.

Date setting is not new. From the time of the Early Church until now, there have been thousands of date-setting, date-suggesting, and date-hinting schemes. All wrong. Now, there are books and pamphlets circulating *proving* that Jesus will come in every year from now until the year 2001.

I firmly believe Jesus is coming back. Over 300 Bible prophecies pointed to the first coming of Jesus. They were all fulfilled. The New Testament has 257 references to the future, literal return of Jesus to this planet. They, too, will be fulfilled. No one can destroy the plan of God, but a lot is being done to erode people's confidence in Bible prophecy.

Our Saviour clearly warned: "But of that day and hour knoweth no man, no, not the angels of heaven, but my Father only" (Matt. 24:36). In spite of that plain statement, schemes for dating the Rapture, the beginning of the Millennium, or the end of the world are recycled over and over.

Who Knows and Who Doesn't

On one hand, it can be demonstrated that God gave Israel

timetables, but none were given for the Church. The Church is the hidden mystery that lies between week 69 and week 70 of Daniel's 70-week vision (Dan. 9:24-27).[1] (1 Pet. 1:10-12; 1 Cor. 2:7; Rom. 16:25; Eph. 1:9-10; Eph. 3:1-11; Eph. 5:32; Eph. 6:18; Col. 1:26-27; Col. 2:2; Col. 4:3; and 1 Peter 1:10-12.)

God can set dates, for He is the planner and fulfiller of all future events. He knows everything about the future and when each event will take place. The date of the Rapture is fixed. It is marked on the divine calendar.

If God truly knows the date (He does), then it is fixed and cannot be changed. If it could be changed, then He does not know the date. If He does not know the date, then we have to redefine God and we may as well throw the Bible out the window. Either God is God and is omniscient, or He isn't. Jesus simply forbade us to attempt figuring it out. There is good reason for this.

While Jesus knew it would be over 1,900 years until He would return to earth, He wanted the Church of all ages to live in the light of that hope, and with a healthy anticipation of His coming. Those who die in the faith are not disappointed. They are in the presence of the Lord and will participate in the first resurrection at the time of the Rapture (1 Thess. 4:13-18).

People saved during the early part of the Tribulation will have opportunity to study the Scriptures, hear the teaching of the 144,000 (Rev. 7), and *exactly calculate the day Jesus will set foot on the Mount of Olives.* For, from the time of the abomination of the future temple by the Antichrist (Matt. 24:15-22; Mark 13:14; 2 Thess. 2:3-4; Dan. 9:24-27; 11:31; and 12:11), it will be exactly 1,260 days until Jesus fulfills Zechariah 14:4 when He sets foot on the Mount of Olives on the East of Jerusalem.

The timing of the rapture of the Church, however, is deliberately hidden and forbidden. To pry into this matter is open rebellion against God. It is defiant disobedience.

To prove this, one often hears the Words of Jesus quoted: "But of that day and hour knoweth no man, no, not the angels of heaven, but my Father only" (Matt. 24:36). In verse 42, the Lord exhorts, "Watch therefore: for ye know not what hour your Lord doth come." And in verse 44 He says, "Therefore be ye also ready: for in such an hour as ye think not the Son of man cometh."

The date setters are quick to point out that Jesus merely indicated that we could not know the day nor the hour, that He did not rule out knowing the week, month, or year.

In Mark's Gospel, however, we find the one Scripture that is the date setter's downfall. After repeating the idea stated in Matthew 24:36, Jesus expands the forbidden territory of date setting the Rapture: "Take ye heed, watch and pray: for ye know not when the time is" (Mark 13:33).

You know not when the time is! And, friend, a day is time, a month is time, a week is time, a year is time, and, *You know not when the time is.* This one statement settles it once and for all.

All date setting displays disregard and disrespect for the Words of Jesus. We are commanded to live in anticipation. We are to "take heed," so don't ignore the message. To do so makes you as guilty as the date setter. We are to "watch and pray" (Mark 13:33).

> For the Son of man is as a man taking a far journey, who left his house, and gave authority to his servants, and to every man his work, and commanded the porter to watch. Watch ye therefore: for ye know not when the master of the house cometh, at even, or at midnight, or at the cock-crowing, or in the morning: Lest coming suddenly he find you sleeping. And what I say unto you I say unto all, Watch (Mark 13:34-37).

Do not ignore, nor fantasize, but take heed, watch, and pray. These are commands for all Christians of all time.

How could a Christian living in A.D. 1257 "watch" without the benefit of the date setters? The same as sane, well-informed Christians today watch for His coming while faithfully laboring day by day until He comes back again. Let not our keen daily hope for the Rapture be dulled with useless and disappointing date-setting schemes. Jesus may come today!

When is Jesus coming back? When is the world coming to an end? Too many people think they have this figured out and are recklessly setting dates, publishing erroneous books and pamphlets, and distorting the meaning and purpose of Bible prophecy.

The Purpose of Prophecy

If prophecy is not given for the purpose of figuring out the date of the Second Coming, then what is its purpose? This subject has been exhaustively treated by great expositors of the Word such as John Walvoord, J. Dwight Pentecost, Stanley Horton, Donald Barnhouse, and a host of others. It will not be necessary for me to treat this question in great depth since so much written material is available.

H. L. Wilmington points out in his book, *Manuscript*, that prophecy proves the Bible is accurate. Hundreds of details of the prophetic word have already been fulfilled. This historic witness demonstrates the reliability of God's Word and the surety of the completion of His declared plans.

Prophecy proves that our existence is not meaningless. The existentialist philosopher may say, "The universe is a red-mawed beast grinding up the flesh of man and beast only to spew them out into an abyss of nothingness." The believer in Jesus says, "My life has purpose. It therefore has value and dignity. I will stand one day before the King of the universe for an evaluation of my life and performance. What I invest in this life accrues interest for eternity. We are saved by faith, but we will be rewarded for good works."

Bible prophecy promotes missions. Not knowing the time of the end, we are spurred on to greater effort in winning a lost world to Christ. In the church I attend, Evangelist Lowell Lundstrom stirred us with a powerful end-times message — challenging us to feed the hungry, visit those in prison, minister to the sick, share the gospel in deed as well as in word. Evangelical premillennialists have stood at the forefront of world missions outreach. We are not escapists, and our record of Bible based activism proves it.

We believe in studying the plan of God so we can intelligently implement His purpose on earth in our time. We do not labor to change the will of God, nor to thwart the will of God, but to cooperate with the revealed will of God. We are the first to shout from the housetops, "Faith without works is dead."

Prophecy is a call to spiritual warfare against the dark powers. *Prophecy is a call to intercessory prayer.*

Above all, *prophecy glorifies Jesus and directs worship to God* (Rev. 19:10).

Prophecy gives us hope for the future. Paul writes that we are "Looking for that blessed hope, and the glorious appearing of the great God and our Saviour Jesus Christ." Note that the Apostle prefaces this Word with an exhortation that we should live a sober, righteous, and godly lifestyle, "in this present world." He continues after the blessed hope passage to urge us on to a life manifesting a zeal for good works (Titus 2:11-15).

Maybe Today!

All date-setting schemes, historically, have proven to be false prophecy, and have always brought disgrace upon not only the perpetrators but upon the Evangelical churches. By quoting biblical "proof" texts, date setters achieve an aura of authority that is impressive in the eyes of their misinformed or gullible followers.

We believe that the coming of Jesus is potentially imminent. Only God knows the exact time of the return of our Lord. But, He knows. To God, the idea of imminence is irrelevant.

To us humans, however, not knowing the time of Jesus' return makes imminence meaningful and a stimulus to holy living as we await. Not knowing the time of His return, we are mandated to work to improve the quality of life, wage war against evil, and carry out the Great Commission as if He were not even coming in our lifetime. Jesus may come today!

Date setting destroys the possible imminence of Christ's return. If I know Christ will return on September 25, then I do not have to look for Him today. It is the date setter, not the continual anticipator who will be caught off guard. Further, it is the unfaithful servant who says, "My Lord delayeth His coming."

Date setters, on the other hand, are saying, "Jesus will delay until the date I have calculated" (Matt. 24:42-51).

I must believe that Jesus could come today, and I must work each day knowing that I may finish out my natural life before He returns. Correct understanding of premillennialism never promotes escapism or irresponsibility.

Polishing Brass and Planting Trees

Back in the 1920s, a cliché became popular in fundamentalist circles. Believing that the world is beyond hope and that we should only live for the Second Coming, many said, "There's no use polishing brass on a sinking ship."

Well, we may just have to live a while longer on this sinking ship, which has been sinking since the fall of Adam in the Garden of Eden. Thank God, there have been a few responsible people who have been "polishing brass," working to improve the quality of life in the present season.

When I was a teenager, I heard about the threat of blister rust to the white pine trees in Montana. My buddy, John Heier, and I hitchhiked out to Troy, Montana, to join hands with the forestry service and spend the summer fighting blister rust. Our team saved thousands of trees.

Each year, I plant trees with my own hands. We have pledged to plant 10,000 trees near the Sea of Galilee at our Christians United for Israel forest. So far, my friends and I have planted over 5,000 trees there.

You can complain about the environmental movement being dominated by New Agers all you want. I will simply ask, "Why did they get the chance to do so? Why were you not out there doing what God has ordered us to do — to care for the planetary home He has given us?"

Bible prophecy, properly understood, makes us the most responsible citizens possible both for this world and for the world to come.

When we speak out against escapism and date setting, we are not undertaking a mere intellectual exercise. This dating game is dangerous.

Special Revelations?

Most date setter's books are intimidating. Some claim to have a special key, "revealed to them by God." Or, they have spent the last 20 years figuring out the numerology of the Scriptures. Some of these books are very nicely printed, some use scholarly language, and all offer very complicated reasons for the author's conclusion.

In addition, these authors make a claim to exclusivity. Only he or she has figured out the true date. The competition is fierce. One of my colleagues humorously suggested that soon, would-be date setters will have to do a computer search for a date that isn't already taken.

Contradictions are rife. The date setters cannot all be right. The fact is they are all wrong. Even if someone gets it right, he is still wrong to do it (Mark 13:33). You don't even have to read the books and pamphlets to figure that out. If they set a date, they are wrong.

If books and papers of this nature are thrust upon you, you should gently rebuke the purveyors of these errors. We cannot tolerate silence in this matter nor allow a readjustment of their calendar of miscalculation when their schemes fail.

Even though the books by Rapture date setters contain some truth, they are tainted with rebellion and must be avoided. Don't join them in their delusion. Keep yourself free from the degrading bondage and confusion engendered by date setters and the false teaching that *always* accompanies their theories.

Those involved in publishing date-setting literature must repent to the Lord and before the Church. They must repudiate their errors. They must put forth as much published material explaining why they were wrong as they did in promoting their errors.

Don't let anyone brainwash you or put you on a guilt trip. Just accept Jesus' words in Mark 13:33: "Take ye heed, watch and pray: for ye know not when the time is."

Live your life in the light of the blessed hope of His coming. Perhaps it will be today! Work and witness with well laid plans for a long time ahead. You will be ready for His coming, for you will be living in obedience, useful endeavor, and hopeful anticipation.

Which Generation?

Certain forms of date setting are based on an interpretation of Jesus' words in Matthew 24:34: "Verily I say unto you, This generation shall not pass, till all these things be fulfilled."

They say a generation is 40 years. Israel (the fig tree referred to in Matt. 24:32) became a nation in 1948. So, 1948 + 40 = 1988. But, it didn't work did it? Will we ever learn from hundreds of past errors of this nature?

Now, a favorite formula is to start with 1967, year of the

capture of Jerusalem, and add 40 years or whatever they think constitutes the length of a generation. There are several flaws in this superficial reasoning.

First, the generation concept is not that firmly fixed in Scripture. The word generation is not a technical nor scientific term. I am not sure that Exodus with the 40-year generation, nor the Book of Job with the 35-year generation, nor the statement that the days of man are "three score and ten" — indicating a 70-year generation — are to be taken as precisely describing a generation. The date setters choose whichever one fits their scheme.

Secondly, why select 1948 for the year when the "fig tree" (Israel) put forth its leaves? Why not the return of the Jews in the 1880s? Why not the founding of Zionism by Theodore Herzl in Basel, Switzerland, in 1897? Why not the founding of Tel Aviv, the first all-Jewish city in modern times, established in 1909?

A likely year would be 1917 due to two major events: General Allenby's liberation of Jerusalem and Arthur James Balfour's famous declaration that "His Majesty's government view [sic] with favor the establishment in Palestine of a national home for the Jewish people, and will use their best endeavors to facilitate the achievement of the object, it being clearly understood that nothing shall be done which may prejudice the civil and religious rights of existing non-Jewish communities in Palestine, or the rights and political status enjoyed by Jews in any other country." Many felt that surely this must be the budding of the fig tree (Matt. 24:32).

Various date setters chose one or another of those dates as a beginning point for their calculations. All wrong! Wrong! Wrong!

The capture of old Jerusalem by the Israelis in 1967 is considered as a date setting possibility by many, because of the reference to Jerusalem being trodden down until the times of the Gentiles being over (Luke 21:24). They think that the times of the Gentiles are now ended. This could not be right since Revelation 11:2 indicates that one more time, after the Temple is rebuilt, Jerusalem will *again* be trodden of the Gentiles for 42 months.

No, the times of the Gentiles do not end until the "Rock cut out without hands" smites the image of Gentile world rule on the feet (Dan. 2). That takes place at the end of the seven years of tribulation, at the Battle of Armageddon.

May we suggest that it was not our Lord's intention in the Olivet discourse (Matt. 24, 25) to provide a means of fixing the time of His return since He immediately says this would be an impossibility (Mark 13:33).

Thirdly, the word translated "generation" in Greek is "genea" and does not necessarily mean a literal generation. W. E. Vine gives one possible translation of genea as "a race of people." (See *Vine's Expository Dictionary of New Testament Words*. Look under the entries: generation, kind, age, and all relevant cross references.)

There are scholars who agree on that translation. If that is correct, then Jesus is simply declaring the indestructibility of the Jewish people. This would be allowable in the context of Matthew 24. He is simply saying that this nation, or race, the fig tree people, Israel will not be destroyed, all these things will be fulfilled.

How About 1994?

Date setters in the Church who claim biblical authority can potentially play havoc with the credibility of the Second Coming message in the minds of millions. Not only the prophecy message will be hurt, there will be a general, negative fallout affecting the entire realm of evangelicalism. When people are disappointed with date setting failures, they are tempted to "throw out the baby with the bath water."

Their downfall is in not being able to distinguish between the valid message of Christ's coming and the perversion as it is perpetrated by false shepherds, opportunists, and the sincerely deluded. We understand that many date setters are sincere, dedicated Christians who love Jesus and long for His coming. But they are wrong, and once enlightened as to the error of their ways, they need to repent and repudiate their teaching.

Harold Camping's book, *1994?* is preparing the way for more disappointment and disillusionment.

Camping is founder and owner of the Family Radio Network of California. Some say he is heard daily by more Christians than any other man. At present, his voice is the predominant radio voice in Russia, Nigeria, and some other countries in

Africa. He has been viewed as a model of stability and Evangelical reliability for many years.

Harold Camping asserts the following:

1. The coming of Christ and the end of the world will take place between September 15 and September 27, 1994.

2. The church age ended on the Feast of Pentecost in the spring of 1988. On May 22, 1988, the loosing of Satan took place and the Tribulation began. The Tribulation is only six years in length.

3. God no longer approves of the Church but will allow the devil to destroy it.

4. God is no longer using the Church or speaking to us through our pastors. "True believers" will get out of the Church.

5. God will destroy the Church by allowing the devil to motivate the Pentecostal manifestation of speaking in tongues. Camping claims that speaking in tongues is the forbidden fruit of the last days, and Satan will bring about a fall just as he did with Adam and Eve and the forbidden fruit in Genesis.

True believers who do not leave the churches voluntarily will be "killed" by Satan. This does not mean that they will be put to death, but that they will be driven out of the church by those who remain in the church. While Camping condemns dreams, visions, and revelations in the churches, nevertheless, on page 322 of his book, *1994?* he says, ". . . many new truths will be revealed to believers very near the end of time."

6. No one can be saved after September 6, 1994.

What will that do to missions giving if Camping gains influence over any more of our people? We know from reports of some Evangelical pastors that many Christians are faithfully supporting Family Radio and have done so for many years.

The book *1994?* is being sold not only over the airwaves and in religious bookstores, but also by Waldenbooks, B. Dalton, etc. The publisher is reluctant to give out numbers of copies sold, but Rev. Scott Temple, an Assembly of God pastor in New Jersey, found out that several editions have been printed in a short period of time. I do not know what Camping's motivation is, and I suppose he is very sincere, but he is wrong, and will do a lot of damage.[2]

An Eastern U.S. book publisher told me, "If you want to

write a best seller in the field of prophecy, name the Antichrist

If Jesus does not come back by the year 2000, it will be the same old story. My friends, Hal Lindsey, Grant Jeffrey, Tim LaHaye, Peter LaLonde, John Wesley White, and other colleagues, may have to consider a readjustment of emphasis! Who will want to listen to us? It is not that the message of the Second Coming is flawed, but that its credibility could almost be destroyed by professed friends of the message — the date setters.

What should the Church do in these crucial times?

The answer for pastors and religious leaders is not to be faint hearted and ignore the subject of eschatology altogether. The answer is not to bow before the onslaught of the dominionists and their ilk. The answer is to preach and teach our message in a responsible fashion, striving to restore the nobility of the message of our Lord's return.

Is the controversy surrounding Bible prophecy the reason why our Bible colleges and seminaries have all but abandoned the field of eschatology? That is not the answer we need for these momentous times. No, but the truth is the answer.

What Should We Be Preaching?

The writer of the epistle to the Hebrews speaks of the triumph of the kingdom of Christ Jesus (Heb. 10:12-13), of fearful coming judgment (Heb. 10:27), and of the return of our Lord Jesus: "For ye have need of patience, that, after ye have done the will of God, ye might receive the promise. For yet a little while, and he that shall come will come, and will not tarry" (Heb. 10:36-37). He will not tarry!

A lay person recently corrected me on my use of the common terminology, "If the Lord tarries."

That person was right. He will not tarry, and when the set date arrives, He will come. He will come as foreordained by God Almighty on the day fixed in the divine mind, whether the Church has fulfilled its tasks or not, whether ready or not. All the accounts will be settled at the Judgment Seat of Christ (Rom. 14:10; 1 Cor. 3:9-15; and 2 Cor. 5:10).

Between these prophecies in Hebrews 10, there is a sober exhortation:

And let us consider one another to provoke unto

love and to good works: Not forsaking the assembling of ourselves together, as the manner of some is; but exhorting one another: and so much the more, as ye see the day [of Christ's return] approaching (Heb. 10:24-25).

There is no biblical reason for the kind of abuse that prophecy is being subjected to, principally at the hands of those involved in attempting to set a date for the rapture of the Church and the second coming of Jesus Christ. There is abundant reason for teaching prophecy and end-times truth in a responsible manner, as it appears in the Bible, without fantasies, fables, and fakery.

We are now at the point in Church history that, if reliable people do not wake up and rescue the Bible prophecy message from the hands of fanatics, we will see this entire area of theology self-destruct before our eyes. This will have a serious and detrimental effect on the Church. It could even be a principle cause of the "great apostasy" of the end times. It could be a prime mover in effecting social and governmental persecution of the Evangelical church. We could see a serious waning of the influence of biblical Christianity as a result of the misguided efforts of date setters.

We must come to grips with the question: "Does the premillennial understanding of Bible prophecy have a legitimacy apart from date setting?" Some think not. It is my conviction that it does.

While most Bible colleges, seminaries, and some pastors of local churches ignore this subject because of its controversial nature, a small cadre of our colleagues are trying to rescue the message, fully realizing that no one can stop the plan of God from being fulfilled, but knowing that the credibility of the message can be destroyed in people's minds. That could be a great hindrance to the winning of the lost to Christ.

Pastor, understand that we do not wish to be exclusive nor to be viewed as the all time great experts in the field of eschatology. On the contrary, we wish to enlist you in our cause and will do everything we can to strengthen your hands in this end of the age of harvest time.

True and False Prophets

The authors of this book, and others, are the theological guerrilla fighters standing, against all odds, to confront the radical date setters, the dominionist, and Kingdom Now skeptics — a veritable host of formidable enemies arrayed against the message of premillennialism.

We believe in a literal Millennium — the future, visible manifestation of the kingdom of God right here on earth. Before the new heavens and new earth and the eternal state are ushered in, there will be a 1,000 year reign of Messiah Jesus Christ on earth. We challenge the Church to restudy the prophets. Reconsider that over a third of the Bible is cast in the mold of prophecy. It is not a subject to be ignored.

Some who identify themselves as prophets today, however, are scorning the message of Bible prophecy relating to future events. The pattern for prophets is set in the Scripture.

Daniel studied Jeremiah's writings, and the prophets were familiar with the written works that preceded their own proclamations. Jesus, the greatest prophet, demonstrated His knowledge of Torah and the prophets by frequently quoting from them.

Any modern prophet who is ignorant of the Bible prophets is not to be heard nor heeded. They are unworthy of the office they claim. Furthermore, any modern prophet who goes so far as to make fun of Bible prophecy (as so many do) is a false prophet.

There are true prophets in the world today like Janabeth Lachenmacher and David Wilkerson. Billy Graham is another. Through the years I have noted several people fulfilling the prophetic role in the Church. These make no claim to a prophetic office. They simply declare what the Lord gives them, and furthermore, they are knowledgeable and respectful of the Bible prophecy message.

People who attend a seminar and become card-carrying prophets are not like the prophets in the Bible. Those true prophets, with the possible exception of Ezekiel, tried to avoid the office. They felt it was an undesirable burden to be a prophet of the Lord.

But — pastors, evangelists, teachers — please do not neglect the prophecy message because it is too complicated, or because it has been abused by fanatics. Preach the Word. Only truth, strongly declared, overcomes error. I suggest that every pastor furthermore question any prophetic speaker, in depth, to determine his or her attitude on date setting — before allowing them in your pulpit.

Yes, I am calling for an all out boycott against date setting! The message of prophecy is too important to let it be ruined by fanatics, deceivers, and even sincerely deluded people.

I hope Jesus comes back before A.D. 2000. I am ready for Him to come right now. But if we are still here in A.D. 2001, the Bible prophecy message will be just as valid as it is today.

The question is, will anyone be listening?

On the Edge of Eternity

A friend once asked the great evangelist Dwight L. Moody, "Mr. Moody, if you knew Jesus was coming back at six o'clock this evening, what would you do today?"

I am sure the questioner was surprised at Moody's answer for he said, "If I knew Jesus was coming back this evening at six o'clock, this afternoon I would plant apple trees."

This is a beautiful answer.

If you knew Jesus was coming back tonight, what would you do today? If there is something you would feel compelled to rush out and do, then you had better do it, for Jesus might come back tonight! On the other hand, if you are daily living your life in His will, then you would not have to change one thing you are planning to do!

God designed His revelation to us so that we are always living on the edge of eternity, and yet always planning for our future here in this life. Suppose He had revealed the very date of the rapture of the Church 1,900 years ago? I doubt if the Church would even be in existence now. It is good to live in anticipation and make your 5-year and 25-year plans. If the Lord comes before you complete your venture, so be it. We won't mind the interruption in the least!

The moment you set a date for the Coming, you upset this divine balance, and you create havoc and distrust in the body of Christ. I tell you, date setting is a sin and should be denounced from every pulpit as such.

Pastors, if you ignore the subject of prophecy or accept some of the modern reinterpretations of prophecy, you have solved nothing. Only by diligent study of and declaration of the Word of God in this realm will you bring real hope and good works with stability to your flock. Ignore prophecy, and the fanatics and distorters will have a field day.

Nature abhors a vacuum. If you create a spiritual vacuum by ignoring the prophetic Word, false teachers will supply something to fill that void. Watch out, pastor, they are coming for you and your congregation. They have already infiltrated. You will ignore this warning to your own peril.

Jesus said:

Watch therefore; for ye know not what hour your lord doth come. . . . Therefore be ye also ready: for in such an hour as ye think not the Son of man cometh. Who then is that faithful and wise servant, whom his lord hath made ruler over his household, to give them meat in due season? Blessed (happy) is that servant, whom his lord when he cometh shall find so doing (Matt. 24:42-46).

I believe the coming of Jesus is potentially imminent. He could come back today. But He may not. It serves us well to be prepared for either eventuality.

I have believed that fact since I was 10 years old. If you had asked me then if I thought I would live to be a man in the late summertime of life (not autumn yet), I would have said it was highly unlikely. After all, I heard the pastor and the evangelists say that "Jesus is coming soon." But what is soon to a little 10-year-old boy isn't soon to an adult.

The word soon is relative and can mean a lot of things. So, along with "tarry," I have thrown out the word "soon." On the other hand, *He may well come back today.* If not, I shall live in anticipation of His coming while doing the work of the Kingdom.

I will continue to proclaim His coming as potentially imminent. But soon? I am not sure how you define the word soon, and the closer one gets to defining the word, the closer one is to being a date setter. I can only say I believe we are living in the final era of the day of grace, the Church Age.

It is better to live as if Jesus were coming today and yet prepare for the future as if He were not coming for a long time. Then you are ready for time and eternity.

"Rip the Evil" — The June 9, 1994, Prophecy

Even as I write these lines many in the Christian world are waiting with baited breath and eager anticipation for the moment when God will "rip the evil" out of this world.

As you read these lines you will have the advantage of having lived through June 9, 1994 and will know if the prophecy was fulfilled.

Appearing on Christian television, Pastor John J. Hinkle announced that *God spoke to him* saying, "On Thursday, June 9, I will rip the evil out of this world." June 9 falls on a Thursday in 1994, not again for decades. Hinkle concluded that now is the time — 1994 is the year. So strongly did he feel about his revelation, Hinkle said on March 14, 1993: "I bring you this morning the greatest message that the Lord God has ever given me. It is so totally powerful and glorious, and I am so humbled and awed by it that I have prayed with all my heart and mean it with all my soul that *if any word I speak this morning is not directly from the Holy Spirit of God that He would prevent me from speaking it, even by taking my life if necessary,* so that no word would go forth that is not His own and His Word is for the whole world to hear." (Italics mine in this and all following quotations.)

It is not my purpose to question the sincerity of Rev. Hinkle. No one doubts His dedication to the Lord, nor his honest desire to see righteousness triumph. But prophecies are to be tested and evaluated by elders in the Church.

Pastor Hinkle said, ". . . The Lord spoke to me in a very loud, firm voice, as clear as a ringing bell and with such power and clarity there was no way to doubt it. . . . This is the startling message that He gave me, '*On Thursday, June 9. I will rip the evil out of this world.*' There was no doubt that this was the voice of God speaking, but my human mind asked a question, and I asked the Lord, 'Lord, Lord, You said in Your Word that no man would know the hour of the Second Coming.' Instantly the voice spoke and said to me, 'I did not say the Second Coming,' and in that moment I knew it was going to be a great cleansing and *destruction of all evil forces and powers in the world. It is not the Rapture, but God's love and glory overcoming ALL EVIL.*

"... On that day all men will see Him as He truly is and fall on their faces before Him. It will be the fulfillment of the Scriptures that say, 'before Him every knee shall bow and every tongue confess that Jesus Christ is Lord.' "

Hinkle received his revelation in 1993 and wondered because June 9 fell on Wednesday not Thursday. He said, "I thought, *Is Satan trying to play some kind of trick?* But before I could complete the thought, that great wonderful voice spoke again and said, 'Check 1994.' I did and there it was, Thursday, June 9, 1994 . . . millions at that time will say, 'This is our God!' and accept Jesus Christ as Lord and Saviour. . . . In verse 10 [of Isaiah 25] He speaks of overcoming ALL THE EVIL and again let me say that this is not the Second Coming, this is by the revelation of the power and glory of God in Jesus Christ to all the world as a great cleansing [referring to Luke 17:20] . . . when the evil is being taken out, one person taken, one left. . . ."

Out of concern for the Church, I wrote and published the following in May, 1994:

> We are flooded with inquiries relating to this prophecy. If it is from God we are all in favor of it. Anything God does that removes evil from the earth is to be highly desired. Anything we can do to implement His will is to be vigorously undertaken by faith. We are commanded to resist evil in all its heinous forms.

I confess that I do not know what Hinkle's prophecy means. We are being asked many questions. Does "rip the evil" mean that all evil will be removed from earth on June 9? That is what the prophecy says, taken at face value. Will there still be sinners on earth, or will they be killed? On June 10 will abortions still be performed? Will pornography and lust cease? Will Satan be absent from the earth? Will it be the Millennium? Will we no longer be led by the Spirit of God to "resist the devil?" James 4:7 commands us to do just that.

How can this fit into end-time prophecies such as 2 Timothy 3:1-13? "This know also that in the last days perilous times shall come . . . evil men and seducers shall wax worse and worse, deceiving and being deceived."

If on June 10 abortions, pornography, crime, lust, child abuse, unbelief, atheism, anti-Semitism, racism, prejudice, murder, war, and disease continue to plague the human race, and if certain political leaders retain their position and power, many will be forced to conclude that the "rip the evil" prophecy is not valid.

Now that June 9, 1994, is behind us, you can see that while the prophecy was born out of honest desire, it was not fulfilled. Satan is not yet in the abyss, he still leads people astray. We still stand on the front lines doing battle against the evils that beset the Church, Israel, and the Gentile nations. Wars have not ceased.

Every knee has not yet bowed.

The Mafia, dictators, warlords, and crooked politicians are still with us.

We are not in the Millennium.

There will still be an Antichrist and the false prophet (Rev. 13), and 21 judgments will be poured out on the earth during the Tribulation. People will not repent, but will rebel against the God of heaven (Rev. 9:20-21). The battles of Magog and Armageddon still lie ahead. There will be a Millennium, after which Satan will be loosed, a final battle fought, and *then* all evil is removed, a new heaven and a new earth come into being, wherein dwelleth righteousness for all eternity.

But take hope, Christ will come, in His own time. Earth will be delivered from the curse, and we are, "Looking for that blessed hope, the glorious appearing of the great God and our Saviour, Jesus Christ" (Titus 2:13).

An important question is, "What happened on June 10, 1994?" Did those who spread this prophecy have the humility to say, "We were wrong?" Or did you hear, "Oh, we miscalculated. We thought God would rip the evil out of the world on June 9, but now we understand that He started the process, and now we must go forth and conquer the world and take dominion over the nations. Then when we have established the Kingdom and the Church is supreme, the Lord will come back and receive the Kingdom from our hands."

A tape recording exists of our spoken words of Wednesday, May 18, 1994, in Lewiston, Maine, before a congregation of believers. We told the people clearly that the prophecy would fail. This was not done to criticize Pastor Hinkle, whom we understand to be a kindly, humble, and sincere man. We had no desire to rob any Christian of their joy. But, in fact, if your joy is based on prophecies outside the Bible you have no true joy nor solid foundation. Only the written Word of God, in its entirety is a basis for real hope.

I would say the same for Camping's prophecy for September 1994. If the Lord has not come before then, we will know that the prophecy was false on October 1, 1994. Date setters seldom give up, however. They reinterpret, recalculate, and continue to recruit. Out of these failed attempts many cults have been born.

The *Merriam Webster Collegiate Dictionary* defines shock wave, "A compressional wave of high amplitude caused by a shock (as from an earthquake or explosion) to the medium through which the wave travels. A violent often pulsating disturbance or reaction (shock waves of rebellion)."

As we move on toward the year 2000 the prophecy shock waves are going to increase. Few can envision the chaos that lies ahead of us. One will almost need a computer search to find a date that someone has not projected as the day of the Rapture, the Second Coming, or some other event. As people's hopes are built up and then dashed over and over again they will rebel against the entire prophecy message. Jesus may come today. I hope He does. But if He has not appeared by 2001, who will be listening to the true biblical message of His coming? Pastors, evangelists, Bible teachers, and concerned Christians must recapture the message of the end times and re-establish its nobility and credibility by preaching the Word of true hope without the radicalism that is so rapidly increasing all around us in the church world.

Epilogue
by Scott Temple

To Russia with "Does God Love You?"

On a beautiful day in June 1993, I was in the great market of Irkutsk, Siberia. A few of us were sowing the seed of God's Word. We handed out a thousand New Testaments in an hour. What a privilege to feed such hungry souls the pure Word of life! In Russia the fields are white unto harvest.

A Russian showed me a tract in the Russian language. I recognized it as Family Radio's "Does God Love You?" tract written by Harold Camping. On the back was the short wave schedule in Russian. Also, on the back was the announcement about the end of time and where to write for a Russian copy of *1994?* These tracts once offered a Bible, but *1994?* has replaced the Bible.

"When and where did you get this?" I asked the Russian.

"There are other Americans in Irkutsk handing these out today," he replied.

Throughout Irkutsk, we saw a multitude of people holding Camping's tract in their hands. Then we met his missionaries. This group of 38 was Family Radio's first mission team to Siberia. Thousands of Camping's tracts in Russian and Chinese filled their "Family Radio Tours" shoulder bags. They were sowing seeds in the same field as my team. The parable of the wheat and the tares came to my mind.

A man from Iowa told me he had been on four Family Radio mission trips. I told him of my debate with Camping. He said, "We'll see in September whether or not he's right."

"No," I replied, "from what we see in Scripture we know right now that he's wrong."

With great sorrow I think of the great harvest of souls being gathered into churches which Camping has labeled apostate. For when they listen in Russian over short wave to Camping's teachings, they will be deceived into thinking they are worshipping Satan. If they follow his teachings, they will be counseled to leave the church they are finally free to attend. What a shock wave!

Months later, on a cold Moscow night, I was in the home of the president of the largest Christian publishing firm in Russia. I showed him the Russian "Does God Love You?" tract to warn him of Camping's false teachings and prophecies.

He asked me, "Is Harold Camping a tall, thin elderly man?"

"Yes."

"He has been in my office. We have translated *1994?* into Russian. It's camera ready. We're planning to print it next week. He's also given me the names and addresses of thousands of Russians. He is paying me to send a copy of this book to them."

"Brother Alex," I immediately pled, "please do not publish that book."

"Brother Scott," he replied, "there are two ways you can approach this. Either you can try to stop bad books from being printed in Russia, or you can continue distributing as many good books as possible to offset them."

Our ministry, Special Outreach Siberia (S.O.S.), has had remarkable opportunities to distribute Scripture. While it was still the Soviet Union, I received permission from government officials in Siberia to distribute God's Word in the public schools. Through this door which God miraculously opened, Life Publishers distributed the *Book of Life* to over two million public school children in Siberia. Tens of thousands have called upon the name of the Lord for salvation.

Preaching the Word is the Church's primary task. But the Scripture also commands Christians to "contend earnestly for the faith which was once for all delivered to the saints. For certain men have crept in unnoticed" (Jude 3-4).

I appealed to my Russian friend not to print *1994?* "Brother Alex, Jesus taught that although offenses must come, woe to that man through whom they come. People will be harmed by this man's false teaching."

"Well, it's too late to do anything now, my dear brother Scott."

I left Moscow utterly dejected. Back in America I asked others to pray that Alex would not print *1994?* Three weeks later, I was in my church sanctuary talking with two deacons about how sad it was that my friend would help spread this divisive book in Russia.

As we were discussing it, a fax arrived. It was from Natasha, my Russian translator. The first words I read were these, "Alex has decided not to print *1994?* He said he loves you." And I love the Lord who hears our prayers and knows our concerns.

The Bear Debate

With love for the Lord and concern for His church, Bible scholars from various schools of thought have joined together in the unity of the Spirit to reject Camping's doctrines and the error of date setting. Amillennial Calvinist theologians and premillennial Arminian preachers find common ground in seeing the danger and the need for damage control.

Chuck Betters, pastor of the Glasgow Reformed Presbyterian Church in Bear, Delaware, organized a debate attended by 1,200 on May 13 and 14, 1994. Westminster Theological Seminary professor Trempor Longman III and Presbyterian pastor Peter Lillback confronted Camping with many of the errors found in *1994?* and *Are You Ready?* Betters correctly anticipated trouble.

On Friday, May 13, a man blockaded the church driveway with his car. He then handed out leaflets portraying Camping as a false teacher. He was asked to leave by Delaware State Police.

Church "bouncers" were prepared to handle people who got out of hand. They actually had to escort people off the premises on both Friday and Saturday.

A good number of Koreans were there. I sat next to Dae-Woo Lee, the Korean who translated *1994?* into Korean. Lee wrote in the translator's preface, "When I think of the eternal punishment of mankind that may come in September of 1994, I become anxious to have as many people as possible read this book."

"Korean Christianity has been especially polluted by false religion," Lee wrote further. He made the following charge: "Based on the teachings of the Bible, the Full Gospel Church (which is proud and claims to have the largest congregation in the world) and the Unification Church are no different in their rebellion against the Word of God."

The event in Delaware reminded me of what happened in October 1992 when South Korea dispatched 1,500 riot police to control the 20,000 disappointed followers of a Korean date setter. The South Korean government considered banning preaching on the return of Christ. Police and medical personnel were put on alert to prevent Jonestown and Waco style mass suicides.

The atmosphere was tense in the Delaware church sanctuary. On the platform sat Betters as moderator, Longman and Lillback as defenders of the faith, and Camping as the focus of the debate. The information contained in *Shock Wave 2000* was acknowledged to be most helpful for these men who contended with Camping. They spoke the truth in love (Eph. 4:15).

Pastor Betters organized this conference because of the dubious comfort Camping offered him following the tragic 1993 death of his 16-year-old son. As he related it to me, Betters received a phone call from Camping who told him, "You only have 14 months left to grieve."

"That's if you're right," Betters answered.

"I know I'm right," insisted Camping.

Pastor Betters realized that if he were not a mature Christian, this kind of counsel could be devastating. Alarmed, he organized a debate with those who, like Camping, and himself, follow Calvinism and amillennialism.

Camping agreed to attend, even though in *1994?* he wrote that there's no time left for theological debates (p.534). Camping's reluctance to have his conclusions submitted to the rigors of a theological debate is understandable. The debate brought to light how shaky the ground is upon which Camping establishes his doctrines and his dates.

Camping said that some of his dates are founded on circumstantial evidence. For instance, during his discussion on dating the birth of Christ, he used the word "circumstantial" three times in one sentence. But just two sentences later, Camping establishes 7 B.C. as the date of Christ's birth because "God has given us a lot of precise information" (GRPC). (Note: GRPC indicates a quote from the debate tapes as listed in footnote 1.)

A fair-minded person would conclude that a teacher who establishes facts this way is building on sinking sand. Longman and Lillback came to this conclusion. They rejected most of Camping's dates and many of his doctrines.

Longman remarked, "I am utterly certain that Mr. Camping is utterly wrong in his conclusions concerning the timing of the second coming of Christ. Why? Because he uses biblical passages in ways that they were not intended to be used" (GRPC).

Camping stated that "there are three possibilities" for the length of the final Tribulation. Longman responded by noting the "great flexibility that his system gives him. He has given you three different options for how long the Tribulation is going to last. He has chosen the shortest one. If we get to October, one of the options is that the Tribulation is a little longer" (GRPC).

Longman published his own "prophecy" in *New Horizons* magazine in December 1993: "My prophecy is that we have not heard the last of Mr. Camping on this subject. He has the book all set up to claim that he only made a simple error in assuming that the Tribulation would be shortened from 23 years. He has intimated that the end might take place in 2011. My advice to those of us who spent good money on *1994?* is to pass when *2011?* (p. 494-95) hits the bookstores."

At the Bear debate, Longman said, "I respectfully reject Mr. Camping's assertion that Jesus will almost certainly come in September. And therefore, my encouragement to you is to be always ready, tonight, tomorrow, in September, in October, and beyond" (GRPC).

Despite the scholarly and scriptural refutation of Camping, the Bear crowd was clearly behind Camping. The audience seemed to share his apparent disdain for theologians. Most of the questions from the audience were directed against Longman and Lillback for challenging Camping's research. Camping quoted Scripture: "Christ said, 'I will build my Church' " (Matt. 16:18). Then, going outside Scripture, Camping said, "But now Christ has become the enemy of the Church" (GRPC).

Twelve hundred people in Delaware heard Camping make that statement. Hearing that heresy spoken in a church sanctuary was shocking.

Dr. Lillback said, "Great men when they err make big errors, big mistakes" (GRPC).

Where has Camping gone wrong? In his method of Bible interpretation, explained Lillback. He noted that whereas the Bible should be interpreted in a Christ-centered manner, Camping's method is judgment centered. He sees judgment "dripping" off every page of the Bible.

"If you can envision a great big dart board. Right in the middle is the bull's-eye with circles all around," Lillback illustrated. "We must always remember the christocentric character of the Bible. Right in the heart of that dart board is Jesus Christ. If you hit Jesus Christ, you have scored a bull's-eye" (GRPC).

Mr. Camping "is kind of like the person who throws the dart first and then draws the bull's-eye around it later," noted Lillback. He throws "darts at the Bible and (is) not even hitting the target. I believe that happens often in the writings of Mr. Camping on this issue" (GRPC). Camping not only misses the mark, but the target. His methods of interpretation and his conclusions are outside of the Bible.

Christianity Today notes that "John Walvoord, a prophecy expert and former president of Dallas Theological Seminary, has debated Camping on a San Francisco radio station. He said Camping is 'practicing a method of interpretation that no one else recognizes.' "[1]

Uniquely, then, Harold Camping has discovered a system of multiplying numbers to discover the date when Jesus Christ will return.

"But what if this date comes and goes?" a questioner asked Camping. The questioner was concerned about increased government limitations imposed upon Christian broadcasting as a direct result of Camping's failed prophecy. The questioner concluded, "I think this could affect millions of people" (GRPC).

Camping doesn't seem to share this man's concern. On the October 1, 1992, "Open Forum" broadcast he asked, "What if I'm wrong? What great harm has been done?" In Delaware, Camping declared, "This is a no-lose, win-win situation" (GRPC).

Camping claims that his prophetic teaching has helped people get right with God.

"Mr. Camping may feel that it is a win-win situation even if Jesus does not return in September 1994. I must disagree," Lillback asserted. "It is a lose situation for all of us." He challenged Camping for justifying his teaching and prophecy. "But would it be right for a Christian physician to tell every patient you only have two weeks to live so that he would get them to listen to the gospel so that they would believe? Would that trouble you? Of course. Because the end does not justify the means" (GRPC).

Harold Camping reached out to the Bear crowd for sympathy. "Many times I wake up at night thinking, *Who in the world do a I think I am?* Here I am saying to the world, the whole world, that I know the month and the year that Christ is going to return. And I am very well aware that many, many people are listening to what I teach and are influenced by what I teach. So, I become more and more aware of the awesome responsibility that rests with me" (GRPC).

"But," Harold Camping said, "I cannot be responsible for someone out there who goes off the deep end" (GRPC). However, James 3:1 says that teachers "shall receive a stricter judgment." God will hold teachers responsible for the effect they have had upon their listeners.

Why Damage Control Is Needed

How have Harold Camping's followers been affected? Only God knows the damage done by the date-setting schemes of men. That's why God warns so strongly against any attempt to set dates. In the Camping case, we may be seeing only the tip of an iceberg sailing toward an October meltdown. That's why damage control must begin now.

As I sat in the Presbyterian church in Delaware, it was like being on the set of a bad movie in the making. After the debate, I did not hear people talking about the biblical challenges to Camping's teaching. Instead, people were discussing their strategies to further the gospel according to Camping. I felt as though I was a ground floor witness to the launching of a new cultic movement.

One man I spoke with rejoiced upon hearing reports of people quitting jobs and selling homes to follow Camping. "Praise God! I sold my business and trucks in California to serve the Lord until He comes in September," he told me. He was part of a group that drove from California to Delaware to give away two truckloads of date-setting books shipped in from Australia. These books were distributed in the church foyer with Camping's blessings.

A college student from New Jersey told me, "I dropped out so that I could be full-time in the ministry."

"By ministry do you mean handing out the 'Does God Love You?' tract full-time?" I asked.

"Yes, but I like handing this out more. It gets to the point faster," he said, handing me an "Are You Ready?" tract. This young man thinks he is in full-time ministry, but he is actually in a full-scale travesty.

The "Are You Ready?" tract asks, "If Judgment Day is really in September of 1994, why didn't anyone see it in the Bible before?" The tract offers an answer. "During the New Testament era God kept information in the Bible relating to the timing of the end hidden because He wanted His servants to focus on the task of sharing the gospel." The message is shockingly clear: (1) the era of God using churches to send out the gospel is over, and (2) the date of the end can be known and must be shared with the world.

A disclaimer says this tract is from Year of Jubilee Ministries, not affiliated with Family Stations, Inc. It also says, "For biblical answers to many questions listen to: "Open Forum" (a live call-in program heard on Family Radio)." The full network of American Family Radio stations are listed.

After the Bear debate ended, a middle-aged group of men and women met in the church parking lot. They discussed their project of raising $50,000 for an ad campaign in *USA Today*. "We want to design it to appeal to the secular mind," one of Camping's zealots told me.

Camping's prophecy has been getting mainstream media exposure. For instance, in 1993 billboards on Interstate 95 in Philadelphia advertised both the WKDN Family Radio station and that September 1994 would be the end of the world.

Another major ad campaign is being organized by End Times Ministries of Philadelphia. The spent over $4,000 for a half-page ad in the June 5, 1994, *Record,* published in Hackensack, New Jersey. This ad stated that Christ would likely return in September 1994. The ad mentioned that Camping's two books, *1994?* and *Are You Ready?* are available at bookstores or the public library. It also highlighted four Family Radio stations and gave Family Radio's toll-free number.

In Delaware, a young couple wore colorful t-shirts that advertised, "For the great day of His wrath is come, September 1994?" The T-shirt reminded me of the missionary to Bangladesh who told me of the unusual attire of rickshaw taxi drivers there. Many of them wear September 1992 "end of the world" t-shirts from Korea. Why? Because they can buy them so cheaply. Date setting cheapens the holy message of Christ's return.

The September 1994 t-shirt was distributed by a young man attending a Camping cell group in Kevin Brown's home in Philadelphia. "Every Friday evening, 50 Family Radio listeners meet in his basement," *Christianity Today* reported.[2] Another Camping cell group that I know of meets in New Jersey. Apparently, groups like this meet all over the country, especially in cities where Family Radio has a station.

How many of Camping's followers have abandoned their church home to await the end of the world? A woman told my friend that Family Radio is her church. Ten people left Community Gospel Church in Northvale, New Jersey, partly because of Camping's teaching. Thirty souls left the Orthodox Presbyterian Church in Franklin Square, New York, to follow Camping. Only God can number how many hundreds or thousands have become spiritually homeless.

A Blind Date

Many people supporting Camping and his Family Radio network do so even though they do not understand Camping's writings. They would agree with the man I heard call in to "Open Forum" and say, "Brother Camping, I don't understand your book, but I believe you're right!"

"Woe unto me if I would be a blind leader of blind," Camping himself said in Bear (GRPC). Yes, for Jesus identifies date setters as "blind leaders of the blind. And if the blind leads the blind, both will fall into a ditch" (Matt. 15:14). Camping is leading his followers into a ditch extending from now until the unknown time when the Lord will come to judge the living and the dead.

Camping's date-setting teaching multiplies numbers to prove that the end of the world will be in 1994. As we have seen, one result of Camping's multiplying of numbers is the dividing of churches. By contrast, the Bible teaches that until heaven and earth pass away, God's program multiplies churches and rejects division as an abominable sin.

In Delaware a pastor stood up to question Camping's accountability. As a pastor, he said that he approaches the pulpit with a profound sense of responsibility. He recognizes that he could lead 200 people astray. He communicated every word with deep emotion. "I think that Mr. Camping could very well be responsible for a great, serious, devastating crime. My question, in the light of those strong words that I have used, if that should turn out to be the case, what accountability, what discipline, should be applied to our brother?" (GRPC).

Dr. Longman said, "I think it is a very important question."

Dr. Lillback noted, "It is a moot question for us personally. Hopefully, he will submit to the board of directors he has. The devastating aspects that you have mentioned, I do know of people who have quit their jobs, changed their career plans, who have done things that they cannot go back and undo, because of his teaching. For them, their lives will be forever different should the Lord not return. It will be a time of looking back and saying, I trusted, and I was wrong. I pray that their faith may not fail. I pray also that God may restore them to usability" (GRPC).

Will Camping apologize? Will he submit to discipline? It seems less likely than the world ending in September 1994. Camping's position is that he shouldn't have to apologize since date setters before him didn't. There have been "all kinds of books that have been written," Camping told *Christianity Today*. "Were the authors of those books disciplined?" Camping asked.[3]

Can Camping come under biblical discipline? Does Camping honor any authority but his own unique interpretation of the Bible? In the Bible we read that even Jesus Christ acknowledged that He was a man under authority (Luke 7:1-10). But Camping is "a loose cannon," as a high-ranking Family Radio staff member complained. As such, he fires at God's people with an apparent death wish for the Church.

Beyond 1994

What will Camping likely do after September 1994? I asked him what will he say on the "Open Forum" broadcast of September 7, 1994, the day after he says is the last day of salvation. "I don't expect to be able to broadcast, because there will be so much chaos," I recall him saying.

"But what if you can broadcast and someone calls in who wants to repent and be saved?" I asked, "On September 7 will today still be the day of salvation?"

Camping said that he doesn't know what he will say then, but he is sure that God's grace will be sufficient.

Unless Harold Camping repents and recants, he is likely to redefine and redesign. This could lead to a continuation of his false teaching and a magnification of this tragedy beyond 1994.

As previously noted, Dr. Trempor Longman has projected that Camping's post-October explanation may be a continuation of the Tribulation. Joe Maxwell concluded his article in *Christianity Today* by noting, "Some see potential for Camping's group to develop as the Seventh-day Adventists did, revising end-time dates and ultimately becoming another denomination."[4]

Similar to the Seventh-day Adventists, Camping identifies Michael as Jesus Christ, even speculating over Family Radio that Gabriel is God. In Delaware, Camping declared that Christ's work was finished after Pentecost. Finished!? He's still working on me!

B.J. Oropeza, a senior researcher at Christian Research Institute, observes that along with a distorted view of prophecy, "Camping undermines the authority of Christ and the Church while overemphasizing the power of Satan."[5]

Pastor Stephen Meyers of the Kensington Bible Church in Philadelphia asks the pointed question, "Is Camping becoming a cult?" In a letter to me, Meyers noted that the first stage in the development of a cult is "a strong personality. Camping is very dogmatic and authoritative. He always has the only right answer."

B.J. Oropeza wrote, "We are left with the implication that nobody really teaches the truth except him [Camping]."[6]

At the Bear debate, Longman highlighted the danger of Camping's apparent claim of being the only one who is right. Longman couldn't reconcile that whereas Camping says that the New Testament era of sending forth the gospel ended in 1988, people continue to be saved until September 1994. "I don't understand this," Longman said, "unless you think that every church is apostate and only your group alone is getting the gospel message out there" (GRPC).

Meyers also remarked that typically in the formative stages of a cult the followers become even more dogmatic in their teachings and dramatic in their actions than the leader. They abandon their church and form their own groups. They give all their money away.

Meyers predicted that after the initial disappointment diminishes when the world doesn't end in September, "Camping's die-hard followers will remain true to him no matter what he says." After that, we may see a "central organization formed to coordinate all the Bible studies into one group. New theology is formed to explain what happened in 1994. It is now a major cult."

Camping may develop a new theology to explain that what happened in 1994 was not physical and apparent, but spiritual and invisible. He has said on many occasions that he has no back up year to 1994 as the end of the world. "Any other year other than A.D. 1994 must be rejected as having any possibility of being the year of Christ's return" (AYR, p. 316).

Camping's comments on "Open Forum" and the "Family Bible Study" indicate that a spiritualization of end-time events may become the explanation for what didn't happen physically. For instance, whereas he once claimed that the sun would literally darken on September 7, now he is saying this may be a spiritual darkening. The range of interpretive possibilities are limitless.

One frightening scenario that could develop is from Camping's method of giving doctrinal definitions to numbers. This scenario could come from the numbers 17 and 23. "Camping takes a page to explain the subtitle 'The Prerogative of God to use Numbers as He desires' (p. 403). This should be amended to say that it is the prerogative of Harold Camping to use numbers as he desires (and then blame God for it)."[7]

For example, in his books Camping gives extensive coverage to the numbers 17 and 23. He defines 17 as meaning heaven and 23 as judgment. Since the final judgment will be only 6 years instead of 23 "judgment" years, 17 "heaven" years remain. *1994?* even featured an Appendix dealing with this 17-year holdover period. Since Camping defines 17 as heaven, he says that the complete number of elect believers will enter heaven in the year 1994. (AYR, p. 282)

After October 1, Camping may claim to have received additional insight previously unavailable. "Why is the world still here and why didn't Christ appear?" callers to "Open Forum" will certainly ask. The answer could be something like this: The world has ended. No one else can become saved. One-third of all those who were attending churches before the Tribulation have become the final members of God's elect family. Indeed, God's family was taken to heaven, but not in a physical sense. The true believers were taken into a spiritual state of heaven on earth.

Presumably, then, God would have a 17-year purpose for Family Radio: (1) to minister to the elect living on earth, and (2) to declare to the world that no one else can become saved because the last day to be saved was September 6, 1994.

If you are reading this book after October 1, 1994, you know more than we knew when we determined to publish our concerns. We wrote this ahead of time for the sake of God's precious people. You now know whether or not Camping repented and recanted, redefined and redesigned, or if he just acted as if nothing unusual happened.

Historically, we know that bizarre doctrines can be institutionalized after prophecies fail. Historically, the integrity of the gospel has been brought into dishonor by perpetuating the doctrines associated with failed date-setting schemes. More than once, false prophecy has been the genesis of a cultic movement.

I pointed out to Camping that his dates and doctrines are impossible to separate. His tenuous dates and dubious doctrines are intermingled like the materials used to make bricks. Then each conclusion is cemented to every other conclusion.

"Mr. Camping, if we reach October 1, 1994, you will have

to abandon the entire structure you have built and begin building again on a right foundation," I counseled him.

"Not at all," I recall Camping saying. "That would not be necessary. The principles that I teach from Scripture will remain intact."

My prayer is that when his dates fail may his unorthodox doctrines also fall into a rubble of disrepute.

Whether or not a major cult is formed as the direct consequences of Camping's doctrines and dates, the many cultic trends should cause alarm. At 72 years old, Camping is at present the youngest of the three men on Family Radio's board of directors. Is Camping accountable only to these two elderly men? What will happen to America's largest Christian radio network when they retire or pass away?

Christian Research Institute reported that Family Radio may be "in danger of self-destructing, according to high-level sources within the ministry." One staff member voiced his opinion that Camping "believes so intently that Christ will return in 1994 that everything else holds no meaning. His family has turned against him, the church community doesn't support his views, and the majority of staff members here at Family Radio fear that the end just might be near . . . not for the world, but for Family Radio."[8]

Five Redemptive Lessons

First, let us learn once and for all that date setting is always wrong. David Lewis calls date setting a terrible and addictive disease. May the Great Physician inoculate us against this last day's madness!

As for Harold Camping's challenge that we prove another year to be more likely than 1994 for the end of the world, let us refuse to enter that contest. Since the Scripture forbids us to set dates, let us not promote an agenda that is in rebellion to the clear teaching of Scripture.

Second, I have publicly repented of committing the sin of date setting. Camping is wrong when he says that other date setters don't apologize.

One Sunday in September 1988 I gave my congregation many of the 88 reasons why Christ was "very likely" to rapture the Church within a day or two. I began with a disclaimer. "I want to step down from the pulpit because I'm not certain that what I'm going to say is true. I am about 25 percent convinced that Edgar Whisenant is correct and that Christ will come this week. His book, *88 Reasons Why Christ Will Come in 1988*, has challenged me. I hope it challenges you to realize that Christ is really going to come."

Millions of copies of Whisenant's book were distributed. Many Christians succumbed to the siren call and yielded to the temptation. We concluded, "Maybe he's right!"

With a prophetic voice let us now publicly and irrevocably declare, "I will never succumb to even the most convincing date-setting scheme. The Bible commands me not to go beyond what is written. I cannot know the time of the Lord's return."

In 1988 I asked my congregation to forgive me for my zeal without knowledge. If you are a spiritual leader and you have committed sin by giving credence to date setting, you should also publicly repent. You should ask forgiveness of those you misled.

Third, let us learn the danger of theological extremism. Romans 14 teaches that Christians can have different convictions without destructive divisions. Teachers who allow a theological system of biblical interpretation to become lord may misrepresent the Lord of the Bible.

Charles Spurgeon, the nineteenth century London pastor, found a healthy balance between the two most prominent theological systems. He said he was comfortable being labeled either a Calvinistic Arminian, or an Arminian Calvinist. He found good and error in both camps. Brethren, let us lay our systematic theology at the Cross and be reconciled to one another.

The apostle Paul said, "Avoid foolish disputes, genealogies, contentions, and strivings about the law; for they are unprofitable and useless. Reject a divisive man after the first and second admonition, knowing that such a person is warped and sinning, being self-condemned" (Titus 3:9-11).

Fourth, let us be convinced of the Church's victory. God will never forsake His church. God will always counsel His people to gather together in a local church (Heb. 10:24-25). The Church is God's ark of salvation.

Jesus said, "And as it was in the days of Noah, so it will be also in the days of the Son of Man" (Luke 17:26). How was it in the days of Noah? The earth was full of violent men as people refused to obey God's Word. The only safe place on earth was inside the ark. In these perilous times, people need to be in a local church.

What else do we know about the way things were "in the days of Noah"? What do we know about life inside the ark? With many animals on board, we know that Noah's ark was a zoo! Sometimes it must have stunk inside the ark. There must have been some creatures that Noah and his family wished were not in the ark. Sounds like your church doesn't it?

Outside the ark, the rising floodwaters rocked those who were in the ark. But, as they were faithful to remain in the ark, God faithfully kept them safe. Don't let anyone trick you into jumping overboard and abandoning the local church built by the Carpenter from Nazareth.

Camping teaches that God has become the enemy of the Church and is determined to destroy it. But if Camping's view of God is right, then Genesis 8 should record that God destroyed Noah's ark. Can you imagine God sending lightning bolts to destroy the ark as it floated safely above the world? Can you imagine God sinking the ark with a torpedo. Would the God you worship doom those He called into the ark? Only a dark corrupted imagination could envision God destroying the ark or the Church. For the same God who faithfully preserved those in Noah's ark will protect and defend His church. God would never torpedo the ark.

Your local church fellowship is an ark of salvation. The world is being flooded with wickedness. Perilous times have come. God has raised up the Church to stand against the polluted floods of sin. It is the Holy Spirit's power made effective through the Church that restrains sin and withstands wickedness. Despite the problems, shortcomings, and even grievous sins requiring discipline, God's will is still for you and your household to be in a local church.

Fifth, let us be convinced by Harold Camping that Jesus will come quickly. Not because he is right, but because Jesus was right when He said, "many false prophets will rise up and deceive many" (Matt. 24:11). The false teaching and deceptive prophecies of date setters are in themselves a fulfillment of prophecy.

The signs all around us indicate that we may very well be approaching the end of the age. The hope of His soon return is a blessing. But the signs that bless can also curse. Signs are a blessing when God's people look up in expectation of the Lord's return. Signs are a cursing when misguided people look down at a calendar and set dates. Signs are instructive, never definitive. That's why no one will ever know the timing of the Lord's return.

In addition to looking up, Jesus taught His followers to "watch out." The disciples asked, " 'What will be the sign of your coming and of the end of the age?' The first sign among many that Jesus gave His followers was the sign of prophetic deception. Jesus answered, 'Watch out that no one deceives you' " (Matt. 24:2-3;NIV). Let us have grace that we may both "look up" and "watch out," for surely our "redemption draws near" (Luke 21:28).

Won by One

One person can make a difference. Gideon did. Esther did. Jesus did. Never lose hope in the fact that you can make a difference. "Never doubt that a small group of thoughtful, committed people can change the world; indeed, it's the only thing that ever has" (Margaret Mead).

One person helping one person is the essence of Christian love. "Greatness lies not in trying to be somebody, but in trying to help somebody" (Anonymous).

One woman read my article "Beyond 1994" as published in David Lewis' *Jerusalem Courier* and *Prophecy Digest* newspaper. She called me the hour it arrived in the mail. "Please send me the cassette of the debate between you and Harold Camping. I listen to Family Radio every day. I dropped out of church. I need to start attending church again." Lord willing, this woman and her family will get back on board the ark of salvation.

One man was angered when his pastor exposed Camping's errors in a Sunday morning service. An emergency church board meeting was called to meet with him. "After 12 years in this church, I'll have to leave," he told me over the phone.

"Then you will be in fulfillment of Camping's false prophetic teaching," I warned him. My heart was saddened as I heard his wife and children in the background.

"Write this statement down," I challenged him. "Christ has become the enemy of the Church." As we continued speaking he tried to say that I'm opposed to Camping's teachings just because I'm Pentecostal. "That's not the point," I replied. "Go back to that statement you wrote down and repeat it to me."

"Christ has be . . . Christ has become . . . Christ has become," he struggled to say.

"You can't even repeat that statement," I said in amazement. The man was in denial!

False prophecy is a spiritual addiction that entraps. We prayed for this man. After the board meeting, his pastor phoned me. "Thank you for your prayers. It was a really good meeting. Praise the Lord! There is definitely a moving of the Holy Spirit in this man's heart. He realizes that, as he said tonight, he is afraid he has been duped. Jesus is working. It's going to be very precious. I told him not to expect it to happen all at once. Piece by piece God will put it all back together." This man is still struggling and still needs prayer.

The date-setting trap is baited with much truth from the Word of God. And like the ragged jaws of a bear trap it entraps its victim. The trap is sprung on the date set by the false prophet. Those who are still swallowing the bait when the trap is sprung are really caught. They will either be seriously wounded or spiritually immobilized. Warn anyone you know swallowing the date setter's bait to get away from the trap before it's too late.

One Pentecostal pastor phoned me after learning what Camping is saying and writing. He said, "I'll have to take my children out of the Baptist Christian school they attend. I understand that the pastor of that church is a strong Camping supporter." I said that I would pray with him for God's wisdom.

A week later he phoned again. He was convicted by Scripture to meet personally with the Baptist pastor. The result was different that what he expected. The Baptist was shocked when he read Camping's statements. Instead of the Pentecostal pastor taking his children out of the school, the Baptist pastor sent each child home with a handout. Many families were warned about Camping's false teachings as broadcast over Family Radio. One man's obedience to God's Word protected many of God's people.

Ten Redemptive Actions

(1) Write to Family Radio and to the other ministries that broadcast over Family Radio. Express your concerns. Many who support Family Radio financially do so because of programs like "Back to the Bible," "Unshackled," Dr. Joel Nederhood's "Insight," "The Back to God Hour," Dr. Cook's "Walk with the King," "Dr. Barnhouse and the Bible," Dr. James Boice's "10th Presbyterian Church Service," etc. These ministries get free broadcast time over Family Radio.

These ministries give Harold Camping's Family Radio Network credibility. In a sense, they help undergird the ministry of a man who is undermining the churches of the world. A free program guide can be had by calling 1-800-543-1495. You can also request a short wave guide for the U.S. and overseas.

(2) Call in to "Open Forum" yourself to talk to Mr. Camping. Call weeknights from 10 p.m.-11:30 p.m. Eastern Time. The number is 1-800-322-5385. The phone will ring until Camping himself answers. You will be live on the air. Remember to minister to his audience.

(3) For a copy of the 90-minute cassette of the debate between Harold Camping and Scott Temple, contact Englewood Assembly of God, 70 W. Ivy Lane, Englewood, NJ 07631, phone (201) 567-4576. Cost will be $3, postage prepaid, for each cassette. You may want to rebroadcast portions of this over your local Christian station.

(4) Contact New Leaf Press at 1-800-643-9535 to arrange an interview with one of the authors of this book, *Shock Wave 2000.*

(5) If you live in a city where Family Radio has a station, sponsor a newspaper ad offering prayer and support to Camping followers. Try to offer an alternative to the advertising blitz being waged by Camping's supporters.

For instance, the April 15, 1994 Philadelphia *Tribune* had an ad that read, in part, "Attention: Philadelphia area Christians RE: The 1994 Controversy. Most pastors in this area misunderstand Harold Camping's teachings . . . He shows that the Bible points to September 1994, after the 6th, as the end of the world.

. . . This is the most important event since Calvary."

Advertise a discussion or a sermon about the issues involved. Offer counsel and prayer. Have the book *Shock Wave 2000* available. *Christianity Today* wrote in the June 20, 1994, edition, "Scott Temple and others hope to run ad campaigns in major American newspapers offering help to the disillusioned." Contact New Leaf Press or write to me if you will be one of the "others" who will offer practical Christian love.

(6) Get this information to pastors and Christian broadcasters. Publicly rebuke this public disgrace to the Church. Inform foreign missionaries, especially those in Russia, China, Korea, India, Africa, and Latin America. They will appreciate getting the information. Family Radio's mission teams have distributed millions of Camping's tracts worldwide in 10 languages. They refer to 1994 as the likely end of time. And they all give the short wave schedule where Camping's date-setting teachings can be heard in their own native language.

(7) Pray for Camping's soul and for those deceived by false teaching and prophecy. Pray that the ministry of Family Radio may be salvaged for God's purposes.

(8) Study, teach, and preach the prophetic Word of God. "Do not despise prophecies" (1 Thess. 5:20). "We also have the prophetic word made more sure, which you do well to heed as a light that shines in a dark place, until the day dawns and the morning star rises in your hearts" (2 Pet. 1:19). Ask your pastor to recommend a good book on Bible prophecy. Teach and preach more on prophecy, for the "testimony of Jesus is the spirit of prophecy" (Rev. 19:10). False prophetic teaching fills the vacuum left by no prophetic teaching.

(9) Publish an article for your church or denomination warning about date setting. One fine example is the editorial comment published by the Church of the Lutheran Brethren in their *Faith & Fellowship* magazine. Editor David Rinden wrote, "The date setters have been wrong before and others will be wrong again, but don't lose sight of the blessed hope that Jesus will come again. It may be soon. Let us be busy about His work finding the lost and bringing them into the Kingdom. Let's not get bogged down in peripheral and speculative issues. Time is too important for that."[9]

(10) Add your signature to the "Manifesto Against Date Setting" found in Appendix II.

Finally, brethren, keep yourselves in the love of God. God does love you! There's no question about it!

The Epistle of Jude instructs God's people to do three things in response to "persons who cause divisions, not having the Spirit:"

1) Keep praying in the Spirit for strength;

2) Keep working to bring the lost to Christ;

3) Keep praising your God and Saviour, Jesus Christ.

These are sensual persons, who cause divisions, not having the Spirit.

But you, beloved, building yourselves up on your most holy faith, praying in the Holy Spirit, keep yourselves in the love of God, looking for the mercy of our Lord Jesus Christ unto eternal life. And on some have compassion, making a distinction; but others save with fear, pulling them out of the fire, hating even the garment defiled by the flesh.

Now to Him who is able to keep you from stumbling, And to present you faultless Before the presence of His glory with exceeding joy, To God our Saviour, Who alone is wise, Be glory and majesty, Dominion and power, Both now and forever. Amen (Jude 19-25;NKJV).

Appendix I

I testify unto everyone hearing the words of the prophecy of this book, if anyone adds to them, God will add to him the plagues that have been written in this book (Rev. 22:18).

Realizing his inability to prove *from the Bible alone* that Revelation is the last book of the Bible, Camping tries various ways to resolve this problem.

First, Camping has resorted to the claim that Revelation *"has to be"* the last book of the Bible because if it is not, then the command "not to add" in Revelation 22:18 would not have been given by God. (These comments were made on the "Open Forum.") Not only is this circular reasoning and thus automatically invalid, it is also faulty on other counts. Deuteronomy 4:2 also gives a command not to add to God's word. If what Camping says about Revelation 22:18 is true, then the Jews should not have received any more books of the Bible beyond Deuteronomy. Obviously, God himself was not confined by such a prohibition. Deuteronomy 4:2 prohibited any uninspired Jew from adding to God's word, but it did not prohibit God from adding to His word.

Second, Camping has claimed that the phrase, *"prophecy of this book"* which is used in Revelation 22:18 refers to the whole Bible. In his mind, this would curtail those who say that the prohibition in Revelation 22:18 only applies to the Book of Revelation, which, in turn, would allow them to add to the rest of the Bible, not necessarily the Book of Revelation. Camping's argumentation is fallacious since there is no biblical evidence that *"prophecy of this book"* refers to the whole Bible. John refers to *"the words of this prophecy"* when he begins the Revelation (Rev. 1:3) specifying his use of the term *"prophecy"* and to what it is applicable, i.e., his subsequent writing of the Revelation. He also closes the Revelation with, *"the words of the prophecy of this book"* in Revelation 22:7,10 as he sums up the material he just wrote in the book. We might also add that the emphasis on *"book"* in the phrase, *"book of this prophecy"* in Revelation 22:19 coincides with the fact that John was commanded by Jesus to write all that he saw in a *"book"* (Rev. 1:11). Moreover, unlike the rest of the New Testament, Revelation is predominately prophecy about future events. Thus, John has good reason for calling it *"the prophecy of this book"* whereas no other book in the New Testament could carry that designation as well as the Book of Revelation. Further, Revelation is the only book in the New Testament that speaks of catastrophic plagues. John warns in Revelation 22:18 that those who add to the prophecy will become victims of the plagues he has just described in Revelation 9-21. There is a natural connection between the two contexts. To ignore all this evidence in favor of the view that *"prophecy of this book"* refers to the whole Bible is to ignore the context of the Book of Revelation.

Third, Camping has also said that if one insists that Revelation 22:18 does not refer to the whole Bible, the rule of "not adding" would still apply since if one adds to the Book of Revelation (Revelation being part of the Bible) he is thus adding to the Bible. The fallacy in this kind of argumentation is plain. If one adds to *any book* of the Bible it can be said that he is adding to the Bible. It goes without saying that no man has the right to add to any part of the Bible. Thus, it is superfluous to make a special case that one is not allowed to add to the Book of Revelation.

The real issue, which Camping fails to address in all these attempts, is that *God* is not prohibited from giving additional revelation if He desires to do so. Camping blunders by not seeing that the command "not to add," whether it be from Deuteronomy 4:2 or Revelation 22:18, or whether it refers to the whole Bible or just the Book of Revelation, does not limit God from giving additional revelation, rather, it prohibits *man* from adding his own words to God's words, claiming them to be of divine origin. Such man-made additions are a grievous sin that will meet the harshest punishment. Revelation 22:18 does not limit God from giving additional revelation anymore than Deuteronomy 4:2 prohibited him from doing so. This is not to say that God *has* given more revelation, but only that He could if He wanted to.

Finally, since it cannot be proven from the Bible alone that Revelation is the last book of the Bible, then no one knows whether some books of the New Testament were written after the Book of Revelation. If there were, these books would have been "adding" to the Bible since the Bible, despite the statement in Revelation 22:18 "not to add," would not be complete without them. Further, in none of these books is it specified that God could not or would not give extra-biblical revelation.

— Robert Sungenis

Appendix II

Manifesto

Whereas the Scripture clearly says that no man can know the day or hour of the Lord's coming, thus indicating that date setting serves no good purpose,

And whereas date setting has historically always proven to be false prophecy which is damaging to the cause of Christ,

And whereas we are living in the last days and nothing must be allowed to detract from the nobility and power of the message of end-time Bible prophecy,

Therefore we, the undersigned, hereby demand that all date setting and date suggesting cease immediately. Let abstinence from this type of speculation prevail until the Lord comes.

We absolutely must stop this type of activity or there will be few who will take the message of prophecy seriously.

If Jesus should tarry until the year 2000 we envision that by 2001 the message of Bible prophecy will be scorned, attacked, and possibly outlawed by legal means — thus giving the New Age movement a clear field for the introduction of their occult humanist messiah.

Signed:

David Allen Lewis, Author of *Smashing the gates of Hell in the Last Days*

Rev. Dan Betzer, Speaker for *Revivaltime* international radio broadcast

Dr. James D. Brown, Pastor, First Assembly of God, New Orleans, Louisiana

Rev. Vernon Boyer, Associate Pastor, Christian Center Assembly of God, Elmyria, New York

Rev. Robert D. Crabtree, District Superintendent, Ohio Dist. of the Assemblies of God

Rev. George Carroll, Pastor, University Gospel Temple, Windsor, Ontario

Rev. Jess Gibson, Pastor, Cornerstone Church, Springfield, Missouri

Rev. Texe Marrs, Author, *Dark Secrets of the New Age,* Austin, Texas

Rev. Jack Stewart, Pastor, New Life Fellowship, Indianapolis, Indiana

Rev. Hilton Sutton, Mission to America, author of many books on prophecy.

Organizations listed for identity of signatories only.

Inclusion of names here does not imply doctrinal agreement in all areas with other signatories.

Signatories indicate endorsement of this manifesto only. All other materials published by him are the sole responsibility of David Allen Lewis.

New names of Christian leaders are being added daily . If you wish your name to be added, please let us know:

> David Allen Lewis Ministries
> 304 E. Manchester
> Springfield, MO 65810
> (417) 882-6470

We urge all born-again believers to join in this enterprise. Let us join hands to restore the power, purpose, and dignity of the message of Bible prophecy. We are living in the end times and Bible prophecy must be rescued from the hands of irresponisble fanatics. We emphasize our belief in the premillennial coming of Christ, the Rapture of the church, the potential imminence of Christ's return, and that that we are truly living in the end times.

— David Allen Lewis

Appendix III

God Does Love You!

As Harold Camping has led many people astray with his claim to know the timing of Christ's return, so he has led as many people astray with has well-distributed tract entitled "Does God Love You?" In this tract Camping claims that God does not really love the human race nor did Christ die for the sins of the whole world. Camping believes that the statement in John 3:16, "For God so loved the world . . ." does not mean that God loves mankind but that God only loves "His creation."[1] Hence, God is said to "offer" His love but in actuality He hates most of mankind. These beliefs are in direct contradiction to the Bible. As with many of Camping's teachings, he arrives at these false conclusions by failing to synthesize all of the Bible's teaching, and at the same time making certain Scriptures overrule other Scriptures in order to make them fit within his narrow theological perspective. The end result is that, as a whole, Camping distorts the Bible's message of salvation.

The authors of this book want you to be sure that, whoever you are, God does love you! As Scripture plainly teaches, God loves all of us so much that He gave His only begotten Son so that whosoever believes in Him shall not perish but have eternal life (John 3:16). The mere fact that God offers salvation to man shows His undying love for him. God did not qualify His love, rather, while we were *yet sinners* He sent Christ to die for us (Rom. 5:6-8). Christ not only died for us (i.e., those that are now Christians) but He died for the sins of the whole world. (i.e., those that are still unrepentant sinners — 1 John 2:2; 4:14). God loves all of us so much that He desires everyone to be saved, not willing that any should perish (1 Tim. 2:4; 2 Pet. 3:9; Acts 17:27). As Jesus taught us to love our enemies, in doing so we strive to be perfect like our Heavenly Father who, by making His sun to shine on the righteous and unrighteous alike, gives us the example and shows us that He loves all of mankind (Matt. 5:43-48; Acts 14:17; 1 John 4:9-10; Rom. 5:10). While on this earth we can have confidence, based on Scripture, that God indeed loves all people, not just the creation. When we preach the gospel we can boldly tell the non-Christian that indeed God does love him! It is not just an "offer" of love.

Here is where the story turns, however. In giving His love to us, God expects us to love Him in return. Unfortunately, there are many who do not return God's love. Though presently they enjoy the benefits of God's love for mankind, someday He will bring their condemnation to bear when they stand for judgment for all their sins and are sent to eternal damnation (Heb. 9:27; John 3:18; 12:48). Of course, God abhors the evil that men do while they are on earth (Prov. 15:9). But until they die and stand for judgment, God, through His love for them, will give them time to repent of their sins and be saved. Because the gospel is always available, the love of God continues to be manifested to the whole world.

God's Plan of Salvation for Mankind

If, perchance, you have read this book and have never heard the gospel, below is a brief description of God's plan of salvation for mankind so that you can be saved.

The Bible tells us that a long time ago God created the universe and the beings that would inhabit it (Gen. 1-3). God loved His creation and desired that His creatures love and worship Him in return. God especially loved mankind and gave him this beautiful earth as his home. All God asked was that man be obedient to His laws — laws that were not burdensome but only given for the good of man. Unfortunately, one of God's creatures, who became known as the devil or Satan, was jealous of God and the special favor God gave to man. He decided to challenge and destroy God's relationship to man by turning him away from God.

As we all know too well, the devil succeeded in his plot as he caused man to disobey the simple command of God not to eat of a certain tree. This is not a myth. It is as real as real can be. It is where the human drama all began.

When Adam and Eve disobeyed, they brought the curse of God and the infection of sin upon the whole human race. To a great degree, God withdrew from man. No longer would God automatically send His angels to protect man from injury or death. No longer would it be easy to obtain food and shelter and the other necessities of life. No longer could man communicate so readily with God as he was able to talk with Him in the Garden of Eden. Though not totally, God also withdrew from man's soul. He was left with inner knowledge of God written on his heart as well as his conscience to determine good from evil (Rom. 1:19-20; 2:14-15; 7:7-25). With God absent from his soul, man found that he had a natural bent toward evil. Because Adam was the head of the human race, these curses and sinful tendencies were passed down to all the generations of the earth (Rom. 5:19). Not only would he now get sick and eventually die, but if the curse of sin and the condition of man's soul continued unabated, after death man would be totally abandoned by God in hell (2 Thess. 1:6-10).

Though He put severe restrictions on their relationship, God still loved man and He wanted to give him another chance for eternal fellowship. Throughout his time on earth, God continually worked with man to bring him back into union with God (Gen. 6:9; Heb. 1:1; 4:2; 11:1; 1 Pet. 1:10-12). However, as much as He desired to help man, God's divine attribute of justice would not allow Him to excuse man's sin without full retribution (Rom. 3:23-26). Also within God's attributes was the principle of *representation*. Through this principle, one person had brought a curse upon the whole human race, so too, God declared that there only had to be one person who, through his obedience and sacrifice, could take the curse away (Rom. 5:15). That particular person had to be a man since it was man who first sinned. He must also be sinless in order to offer himself a perfect sacrifice for sin (2 Cor. 5:21; Heb. 1-10). Since all of mankind was sinful, there was no one who could fulfill these requirements. God, knowing that there was only one way it could ever be done, decided that

He must become a man himself. Being a mystery indeed, God accomplished this plan through the three divine persons, that is God the Father, God the Son, and God the Holy Spirit. Through agreements with the Father, the Son accepted the role to become the man who would pay for the sins of the whole world (John 1:1; 17:1-26; Acts 2:23). In order to unite His divine nature with a human nature, the Holy Spirit conceived Jesus in the womb of a virgin woman, namely, Mary (Matt. 1:20). Hence, Jesus became the God-man — a unique being that was totally God and totally man, as hard as that is to comprehend. In coming to earth, Jesus' purpose was to restore in even greater splendor the full fellowship between God and man that had been lost in the Garden of Eden.

Before His ultimate goal of atoning for the sins of men was accomplished, throughout His life and ministry Jesus showed great love to man both physically and spiritually, especially by teaching them about God's plan of salvation. In one of His greatest and most succinct teachings Jesus said, *"For God so loved the world that he gave his only begotten Son, that whosoever believes in Him shall not perish but have everlasting life"* (John 3:16). In giving himself for the sins of the whole world, He personally invites each man, woman, and child to believe in Him and His work so that they can live eternally in heaven and escape the eternal abandonment in hell that God will bring upon unrepentant sinners. Throughout the centuries this message of salvation has been preserved and proclaimed through Christ's church so that all people could know the truth (Matt. 16:18-19; 1 Tim. 3:15).

In completing His mission, Jesus suffered and died on a cross as prophesied in Scripture (Gen. 3:15; Luke 24:44). In this way, Jesus atoned for our sins, satisfying the Father's justice (Rom. 2:26). The climax of Jesus' mission was fulfilled when He rose from the dead on the third day. Jesus conquered the curse of death that was given to Adam (Rom. 5:12; 1 Cor. 15:20-58). Because of His resurrection, those who believe in Jesus will also rise from the dead, never to die again (John 6:40).

In setting up this program we understand from Scripture that God's salvation is possible only through His grace (Eph. 2:8-9; Titus 3:3-8). From start to finish, salvation and all its aspects is the work of God. Though God provides all that is necessary to be saved, man must believe in and obey God, bow to Him as Creator and ruler, and repent of his evil ways. Through God's judicial decree and the transforming power of the Holy Spirit, man can become justified before God (Rom. 4:1-26; James 2:20-24). Through God's grace, man is prompted to receive the gift of faith along with the power to perform good works. In His eternal foreknowledge, God had predestined the salvation of man, yet in that foreordained plan He also included the free will of man to accept or reject God (Acts 17:24-31; Matt. 23:37; Luke 22:22; Eph. 1:4-5; John 1:12-13; 6:35-71). In incorporating free will into the redemptive plan, God commands us to work out our salvation with fear and trembling, even as He works in us, never taking His grace for granted (Phil. 2:12; 3:12-16; Eph. 2:10; 1 Cor. 9:27; 10:12-13). Many men will not come to God because they do not want their sins exposed (John 3:19-21), nor do they want to give up their sin (Rom. 1:18). Yet God, through His love of man, continually holds out the offer of salvation, not willing that anyone should perish, but desiring all to repent and obtain salvation (2 Pet. 3:9; 1 Tim. 2:4). Once we believe in God and accept His salvation, then we must also persevere in faith till the end (Matt. 24:12; John 15:2-6; Rom. 11:22; Gal. 5:4; 2 Cor. 6:1-2; 13:5; 1 Tim. 1:18-19; Heb. 6:4-6; 10:29-39). While on this earth God requires us to love our neighbor, both physically and spiritually (2 Tim. 4:2-5; James 1:27; 2:15-17; Rom. 13:9-10; Matt. 25:34-36), and in this way we do His good works and become conformed to the image of His Son (Rom. 8:28-30; 1 Pet. 1:2). We pray unceasingly that God will help us in this life so that we can continue in His grace and obtain the inheritance He so desires to give us (2 Thess. 1:11-12; 3:1-2; Heb. 12-13).

In relation to the theme of this book, we must also add that at some time in the future, a time not known by man, the world will end. Right before the end, Scriptures are explicit that the *"man of sin"* must be revealed (2 Thess. 2:1-12). So far, there has been no one who has assumed this identity. Contrary to Camping's claim, the man of sin is not Satan because Satan is not a man. Rather, this man will appear *"according to the working of Satan"* (2 Thess. 2:9). According to Paul, the man of sin will rule over all that claims to be divine or is worshipped as divine, actually proclaiming himself to be God. In accord with Satan, this religious impostor will sway the whole world with all kinds of miracles, signs, and wonders, most likely offering a solution to humanity's problems and the release from religious persecution in exchange for apostasy from true faith in God. Then Jesus Christ will return in triumph over Satan at the end of the age.

Whether these things will come upon the world very soon or are planned for a long way off, each of us must be prepared to meet God at any time, either at death or the end of the world. In order to be saved we simply have to believe in the Lord Jesus, as Paul told the Philippian jailer (Acts 16:31; Rom. 10:9-11). Faith is an acknowledgment that Jesus is the Son of God and has atoned for our sins (1 John 3:23). Faith works through love and is accompanied by obedience (Gal. 5:6; 1 John 5:1-5; Rom. 1:5; 16:26). Obedience to God requires that we repent of our sins (1 John 1:8-10) and that we do the works that show we love God and our neighbor (Rom. 13:9-10; 1 John 3:23-24). The Scriptures also command us to be baptized, even as the Philippian jailer was baptized the same night he believed (Matt. 28:19; Acts 2:38; 16:33; 1 Pet. 3:21).

Do not delay. Now is the day of salvation. Tomorrow may be too late (2 Cor. 6:2; Luke 12:16-21). Call upon the name of the Lord and receive God's blessed salvation. For it is through faith in the finished work of the Son of God at Calvary that you are made ready for His coming. Are you ready? By God's mercy and grace you can be ready!

— Robert Sungenis

Notes

Prologue

[1]Quote from Harold Camping's comments made at the debate sponsored by the Glasgow Reformed Presbyterian Church, Bear, Delaware, on May 13-14, 1994. The seven-tape series may be ordered by calling the church at (302) 834-GRPC. More information about this debate will be found in the epilogue of this book. For simplicity, future quotes from the May 13-14 debate will be in the text as (GRPC).

[2]Harold Camping, *1994?* (New York, NY: Vantage Press, 1992).

[3]Harold Camping, *Are You Ready?* (New York, NY: Vantage Press, 1993).

[4]Camping, *1994?* p. 169.

[5]Camping, *1994?* p. 180.

[6]Camping, *1994?* p. 186.

[7]From tape transcript of WMCA debate. Cassette available. See further resources.

[8]Camping, *1994?* p. 534.

[9]Camping, *1994?* p. 516.

[10]Camping, *1994?* p. 533.

[11]*Christianity Today,* "End-times Prediction Draws Strong Following," June 10, 1994.

Introduction

[1]For further information on Camping's relationship with the staff at Family Radio, see the article by Perucci Ferraiuolo, "Could *1994?* Be the End of Family Radio?" *Christian Research Journal,* Summer 1993.

[2]Scott Temple, *1994 and Other Date Setting Disasters* (unpublished paper, Englewood, NJ, 1993), p. 12.

[3]Camping, *1994?* p. 533.

[4]My degrees are: *Bachelor of Arts in Religion,* 1980, George Washington University, Washington, DC; *Master of Arts in Religion,* 1982, Westminster Theological Seminary, Philadelphia, PA (Robert Sungenis).

[5]Camping, *1994?* p. 382.

[6]Frank S. Mead, *Handbook of Denominations* (Nashville, TN: Abingdon Press, 1980, 7th ed.) p. 19-20.

Chapter 1

[1]Edgar C. Whisenant, *88 Reasons Why the Rapture Will Occur in 1988* (Edgar C. Whisenant, 1988). Since 1945 there have been over 200 books published that have predicted the timing of the return of Christ. Other end-time predictors include: *Christ Returns by 1988* by Colin Deal; *Get All Excited Jesus Is Coming Soon* (September 6, 1975) by Dr. Charles Taylor; *The End of Time, The Messiah Comes* (April 1, 1981) by Elijah Two; *The Midnight Cry* (the present era ends by 1980) by Mikkel Dahl *The First 7,000 Years,* (the millennium begins in September, 1996) by C.G. Ozanne; *Soon Coming World-Shaking Events, Armageddon Before A.D. 2000* by Christian Missionary Society; *The Late Great Planet Earth,* by Hal Lindsey.

[2]Harold Camping, *The Fig Tree* (Oakland, CA: Family Stations, Inc., 1983).

Chapter 2

[1]Ernest Springer, *Argument for a Fair Hearing* (Audubon, NJ: Old Path Publications, 1994), p. 10-11.

Chapter 3

[1]Harold Camping, *Adam When: A Biblical Solution to the Timetable of Mankind* (Alameda, CA: Frontiers for Christ, 1974. Revised edition: Oakland, CA: Family Stations, Inc., nd).

[2]Edwin Thiele, *Chronology of the Hebrew Kings* (Grand Rapids, MI: Zondervan Publishing House, 1977).

Chapter 4

[1]J. William Whiston, trans., *Josephus: Complete Works; Antiquities of the Jews,* book xvii, chapter vi, number 4, p. 365 (Grand Rapids, MI: Kregal Publications, 1960, 1978, 1981).

Chapter 5

[1]Springer, *Argument for a Fair Hearing*, p. 38.

Chapter 8

[1]Bruno Kolberg, *The Final Tribulation . . . Days of Vengeance* (Brisbane, Australia:Bruno Kolberg, 1993).

Chapter 10

[1]Temple, *1994 and Other Date Setting Disasters,* p. 30.

Chapter 11

[1]Gyles Brandreth, *Number Play* (New York, NY: Rawson Associates, 1984).

[2]Milton S. Terry, *Biblical Hermeneutics* (Grand Rapids, MI: Zondervan Publishing, 1974), p. 384-385.

Chapter 14

[1]Harold Camping, *What God Hath Joined Together* (Oakland, CA: Family Stations, Inc., 1985), p. 36.

[2]Harold Camping, *First Principles of Bible Study* (Oakland, CA: Family Stations, Inc., 1986) p. 29-30.

[3]Camping, *First Principles of Bible Study,* p. 45-52. See also p. 17 of *1994?*

[4]Thomas Schaff, *Personal Bible Study,* (published by Family Radio School of the Bible, no date given).

Chapter 15

[1]Robert Anderson, *The Coming Prince* (Grand Rapids, MI: Kregel Publications, 1979), 14th edition, p. 4.

[2]Camping, *1994?*

Epilogue

[1]*Christianity Today,* "End-time Prediction . . ." June 20, 1994.

[2]*Christianity Today,* "End-time Prediction . . ." June 20, 1994.

[3]*Christianity Today,* "End-time Prediction . . ." June 20, 1994.

[4]*Christianity Today,* "End-time Prediction . . ." June 20, 1994.

[5]B.J. Oropeza, "The Late Great Credibility of Harold Camping" research paper (San Juan Capistrano, CA: Christian Research Institute). Also note book by B.J. Oropeza, *99 Reasons Why No One Knows When Christ Will Return* (IVP, 1994).

[6]B.J. Oropeza, "The Late Great Credibility of Harold Camping."

[7]Stephen C. Meyers, "1994?" *Christian Research Journal,* Winter 1994.

[8]Perucci Ferraiulolo, "Could *1994?* Be the End of Family Radio?" *Christian Research Journal,* Summer 1993.

[9]David Rinden, "1994?" *Faith & Fellowship,* November 20, 1992.

Appendix III

[1]Harold Camping, *God's Magnificent Salvation Plan* (Oakland, CA: Family Stations, 1981), p. 42. Though not in this book, in his Bible studies Camping teaches that God hates mankind, based on verses such as Psalm 5:5; 11:5.

Sources For Further Study

Carson, D.A., *Exegetical Fallacies* (Grand Rapids, MI: Baker Book House 1984).

DeMar, Gary, *Last Day Madness* (Brentwood, TN: Wolgemuth and Hyatt Publishers, 1991).

Ferraiuolo, Perucci, *Christian Research Journal*, "Could *1994?* Be the End of Family Radio," Summer 1993, San Juan Capistrano, CA.

Fisher, Richard G., *The Quarterly Journal*, "Will Jesus Return in 1994? — The Prognostications of Harold Camping," Vol. 13, No. 1, January-March 1993.

Green, J.P., *The Christian Literature World*, "1994 — 22 More Months to Live! Are You Ready?" Vol. IV, No. 3-4, Fall-Winter 1992.

Guske, Robert J., *Random Musings*, "To Date or Not to Date," December 1993.

Isbell, Sherman, *The Presbyterian Reformed Magazine*, "Predicting Jesus' Return: A Review of Harold Camping's *1994?*" Fall 1993, Vienna, VA.

Jordan, James B., Institute for Christian Economics, "Biblical Chronology: *1994?* — Not!" Vol 5. No. 7, November 1993.

Klett, Fred, *Manassas*, "The Great Fig Tree Fallacy," Vol. 171, No. 1, January 1993.

Kolberg, Bruno, *The Final Tribulation . . . Days of Vengeance* (Brisbane, Australia: Bruno Kolberg, 1993).

Longman, Tremper III, *New Horizons in the Orthodox Presbyterian Church*, "1994: The Year of Christ's Return? A Review of *1994?* by Harold Camping," Vol. 14, No. 10, December 1993, Horsham.

Mead, Frank S., *Handbook of Denominations* (Nashville, TN: Abingdon Press, 1980, 7th ed.).

Meyers, Stephen C., *Christian Research Journal*, *"1994?"* Winter 1994.

Noe, John, *The Apocalypse Conspiracy* (Brentwood, TN: Wolgemuth and Hyatt Publishers, 1991).

Oropeza, B.J., *The Late Great Credibility of Harold Camping* (unpublished paper from the Christian Research Institute, 12 pages).

Springer, Ernest, *"1994?" — Argument for a Fair Hearing* (Audubon, NJ: Old Path Publications, 1994)

Temple, Scott, *1994 and Other Date-Setting Disasters* (unpublished paper, Englewood, NJ, 1993) Tapes of the debate between Temple and Camping are available upon request. Write to Pastor Scott Temple, 70 West Ivy Lane, Englewood, NJ 07631.

Terry, Milton S. *Biblical Hermeneutics* (Grand Rapids, MI: Zondervan Publishing House, 1974).

Venema, Cornelius P., *The Outlook*, *"1994?* Another Misguided Attempt to Date the Return of Our Lord" Vol. 43, No. 8, September 1993, Byron Center.

West, Jim, *The Two Edged Sword*, "Harold Camping's View on the Return of Christ, Probably in 1994," Vol. 7, No. 1, January-February 1993, Sacramento.